Abby's Road, the Long and Winding Road to Adoption

And how Facebook, Aquaman and Theodore Roosevelt helped

MICHAEL CURRY

ISBN: 0692221530
ISBN 13: 9780692221532
Library of Congress Control Number: 2014909963
Curry Books
Mount Vernon, IL MO 5/29

Dedication

This book is dedicated to Valerie and Jonathan (not their real names). If we could give you all the stars in the sky it would not be enough to thank you for your wonderful gift. Rest assured we love our little girl with all our hearts and minds and souls and there will never be a day she will not know about your love for her.

Speaking of love, this book is also dedicated to my two pretty ladies: Esther, whom I love more than life itself; and Abigail. This is all for you, my baby doll.

Table of Contents

Introduction

"The Baby Story" is our daughter's favorite bedtime story. She knows it so well she can repeat it to us. It has the added benefit of being true.

"Once upon a time, there was a mommy and a daddy who loved each other very much. And they wanted to have a baby of their very own, but they couldn't even though they tried and they tried.

"So they decided to adopt a baby. They talked to some very nice people who help mommies and daddies like them.

"And they met a very nice man and woman named Valerie and Jonathan who were having a baby but couldn't be the baby's mommy and daddy. So they picked Mommy and Daddy to be their baby's mommy and daddy.

"So when it came time for the baby to be born, the mommy and daddy took a long plane ride to Long Island, New York where they waited and waited, and they waited and waited, and they waited and waited until finally the baby was born.

"The next day they went to the hospital to see the baby, but they couldn't hold her. They could only look at her through the nursery window lying in her teeny tiny little baby bed. But the day after that they got to go back.

"They got to hold the baby. They got to dress the baby. They got to name the baby Abigail, put her in a car seat, put her in the car and take her back to the hotel where they were staying.

"And after a few more days they took a long train ride home where they lived happily ever after.

"The End."

Prologue

I am the father of a newborn baby. I am 45 years old. "What are you think-ing," my friends will say, "are you insane?"

At 45 I should be near the end of my parenting. My first children are at long last grown and gone. The children still around are so independent they shout from the door, "I'm leaving; I'll be back when I'm damn good and ready."

"Okay," I would call back from the living room.

At 45 I should be jumping for joy because I dropped my kids from my auto insurance; that alone makes up for the loss of the deduction on my income tax when they turn 18.

Oh, I'll still help the kids, sure. A few bucks here or there to help make ends meet. The odd meal once a week at the house, maybe co-signing for a car-that-you-better-pay-every-month-if-I-even-think-you-are-a-day-behind-that-car-is-mine-do-you-hear? But no more school bills, no more empty refrig-erators the day after we just went shopping ... we can take that long vacation out west. Or east! Or a cruise!

And the kids will just have to fend for themselves!

Do you want to go see a movie? It would be nice to watch the latest Spider-man flick on the big screen, wouldn't it? And we can go out to eat afterwards!

At 45 I may even be preparing to become a grandparent. What? That's not possible! Can't he call me "Uncle Mike" instead of "Grandpa"? Grandparents are in their 50s or 60s not their mid-forties; too soon, too soon. But what a sweet little baby, grandpa's little man. Oh don't cry; there there. Ooo! Stinky diaper! Let me give you back to your mother. Or father. As long as I can pass him off to somebody else…

At 45 what I should NOT be doing is getting up every two hours for feeding, watching Barney, paying for daycare, watching Barney, potty training, watching Barney, putting up with temper tantrums, watching Barney Barney Barney.

But I am not just a father at 45; I am a new father at 45. "Never mind," my friends will say, "you ARE insane!"

At 45 I should not be, for the first time, getting up every two hours for feeding, paying for daycare, potty training, putting up with temper tantrums-when-there-is-no-logical-reason-in-the-world-to-go-so-ballistic and who's Barney?

I'll be sixty when she goes to prom; I'll be 63 when she graduates high school, 67 when she graduates college if she's lucky enough to finish in four years.

By the time I teach her to drive, I'll be an old man; and driving like an old man. "Go ahead and pull out, they'll stop. Gauge how fast the oncoming traffic is coming so you can go slower than that. He has finally passed us after ten minutes; when he gets back into the driving lane, turn at the next right. You did very well, dear, here's your trilby."

And yet here I am, one month away from my 46th birthday with a little living baby doll snuggled on my chest. She's so warm and cuddly and I love kissing her little forehead and listening to her coo and sigh. The hysterics will come soon enough. Right now we are a happy and sweet family of three. And, yes, I know it's uphill from here, but it's already been quite a climb. Right now I can sit on the plateau and enjoy the view.

One

WHAT IS PAST ...

*E*sther and I married in the year 2000, along with everyone else in the world, so it seemed. Party supply stores and bridal shops I spoke to said their demand was constant and supplies dwindled even just after delivery days. There were 2.3 million marriages in 2000 and more than that married in 2001. The numbers decreased through the decade but only by 200,000 (2.096 million in 2010 for example).

It was my first marriage, her second.

On November 8, 1999, my secretary told me Esther was on the phone - line one. I knew she was going to ask me out on a date. How I knew that I don't know – but in our lives together we very often finish each others' sentences, think the same thoughts – "do you want to get a pizza for dinner?" "You've read my mind." – that sort of thing.

She was, and is, very cute and sweet and the most kind and gentle soul I have ever known. And also very strong and brave (strong and gentle seem to go together, don't they?). Our first date was on Friday November 12th. Our second the 13th. By the day after Thanksgiving I knew I was in love with her.

The day after Thanksgiving was also the last time I spent an entire day without seeing her or talking to her on the phone. I proposed New Year's Day 2000 and we married that September.

I am an attorney and she is a librarian. I know three other attorneys who are also married to librarians. There must be something in the temperaments of those professions that get along well.

I don't remember when we decided to have children. At no point did one of us tell the other, "Let us conceive." But we must have talked about it, because decide we did.

Why did we decide to go from a family of two into a family of three, four or five? It's easy for me to say it was because I love the idea of there being more people like Esther in the world, but it goes deeper than that. Our reasons grew over the nine years of our marriage before Abby.

Legacy was an original reason: someone to remember us - to tell their children and grandchildren about. "Here's a photo of your great-grandmother, she worked at a library." "These are birthday cards your grandparents sent to each other." "That's your great-great grandfather's signature on that Petition."

Another reason came later: who would care for us in our dotage? When one of us dies, who will take care of the other? This reason came after Esther's mother died in 2006. If I were gone, who would be there to pat Esther's hand and sit with her and talk to her in the hospital bed?

I wanted someone to take care of me in my old age, too. I took a more practical approach: "I changed your diaper, now you change mine!"

I think the main reason was we were both lonely. I love my wife and to this day prefer her company to anyone else's. She is my best friend and I am hers. But it was just the two of us in our house. We wanted little ones running around. My love for Esther overflows and I wanted someone else on whom I could pour my love. The two of us were so happy, imagine three of us. Or four!

When we first married Esther did not believe in the concept of "soul mate" – a couple so linked emotionally, spiritually and intimately that it seems unnatural for them not to be together. I called Esther my soul mate from the moment we were engaged.

Esther did not call me her soul mate until a few years into our marriage. Up until then she didn't believe in soul mates. I didn't mind. It was probably because she had been married before. When she divorced her belief in a soul mate fizzled. After she realized how similar our tastes and how compatible our differences, though, she believed in soul mates.

She didn't believe in best friends either. She believes in that now, too.

2

Think of all the wrong reasons couples have a child — to save their marriage or to strengthen weakening bonds. Sometimes it works. Sometimes it makes things worse. Our marriage didn't need saving; our bonds weren't weak. We loved each other and we wanted someone else to love too. So we decided to have a baby.

The importance of research was pounded into me in law school from day one. Plus I was always bookish. Esther is a librarian and loves reading as much as I, plus she had access to every book ever written. Well, every book ever written as long as it was in the library system.

So we studied and researched and applied what we learned to get pregnant.

We took vitamins. Mine was a supplement designed for women: I took so much zinc I picked up cell phone signals in my fillings. We ate food that made for strong sperm and receptive ova. We kept a calendar and took Esther's temperature three times per day.

"We only have ten minutes! Hurry, hurry! We'll have dinner later!" At times I barely had time to remove my tie.

And sometimes we would miss the ovulation window altogether. We'd each be at work or she would ovulate in the wee morning hours.

But when her temperature went up (spiked), that meant she had ovulated. We missed our chance. Maybe next month. Then the month after. Then the month after…

It wasn't working.

At the time Illinois state law mandated insurance coverage for infertility treatments. Insurance companies for businesses employing over a certain number have to cover infertility treatment as if it were a medical condition (which it is). The logic is thus: if they cover for erectile dysfunction, they have to cover infertility. Tit for tat; so to speak… Whether they still have such a law I do not know.

Self-help was not working. Let's see if modern medicine would.

Esther was given pills that would help create a litter of 6 kids or so.

I was given Levitra to help the old soldier stand and salute.

One side effect was intense drowsiness. Much like taking Nyquil, I'd best be sitting down when I took my Levitra otherwise I'd wake up on the floor. The drowsiness was all right, though. It didn't matter. I didn't have to be awake; I just had to be there.

"That was BC." "Of course, all this happened BC." Before Children. It's one of those phrases you never knew existed until you hear it from other parents.

They have their own language, parents do; their own code words. And they always hang out with each other. It's like a cult.

I add my own: BE – before Esther. BE, I was able to pack for a weekend getaway with a small duffle bag. Pants, socks, shirt, 2 pair of underwear, t-shirt and shorts to sleep in, toiletries and my pillow. I always take my pillow. My mother made it for me out of three separate feather pillows. It's as hard as a cinder block and nearly as heavy. And that's all I needed to travel. I went to London for ten days with one duffle bag. Through Heathrow with one carry-on – that's the way to go.

AE – After Esther, I could still manage one duffle bag. She needed a big suitcase. Sometimes two. AC – After child, the baggage grew exponentially. When we walked through a motel lobby you'd think Cirque du Soleil was in town. Two suitcases, a cooler, a folding crib, a portable DVD player with her nighty-night music CDs (we now have I-pods, pads and such…), another case filled with toys and books, the diaper bag, Esther's purse that has also grown exponentially during the life of our marriage. Then my old duffle bag crammed into the floor of the back seat or smooshed in the back of the trunk, forgotten.

Esther was attacked by fibroids. "Weren't they bad guys from a Patrick Troughton-era *Doctor Who* episode?" I asked. No, they were thingies that grew on the inside of lady parts and interfered with pregnancy. Well then, if that's the cause of our problems, out they go!

Our adventure to St. John's Hospital to fight the nefarious fibroids was between AE and BC, so we only had the two suitcases, plus her purse and my duffle bag. We stayed overnight at a nice motel, ate an early dinner, read, watched TV and then to bed. Up early the next morning through the St. Louis traffic to the hospital for an 8:00 am out-patient procedure.

Esther sat in a wheelchair and an intern took her through swinging doors leading to inner chambers. The waiting area was a big circular balcony overlooking the lobby with its huge water fountain. I sat in a quiet spot and read the paperback I had brought. Several hours later the doctor came and asked me to join him through the swinging doors.

He said the operation went well and started showing me x-rays. "There are the fibroids," he said and pointed at several white blotches on the black and white pictures.

It was like those 3D pictures that were so popular in the 1980s. A crowd gathered in front of a store in the mall. Everyone stared at a framed picture of little blue or red dots. Eventually someone would walk up and point and say, "Oh, a space shuttle, see? And this one has dolphins, right there. You just gotta unfocus your eyes." Everyone would ooh and aah and say "Oh yes, there it is" and fork over their money for the pictures. I never saw it. What I did see was that same guy pointing to the shuttle and the dolphins the next week. I'd bet later in the day he puts his name tag on and gets back behind the register. He's a shill. It's a confidence game – not only am I out the money but now I've got crossed eyes.

Back to the x-ray: "There are some fibroids outside the uterus," the doctor was pointing at some white spots on the edge of what looked like a map of the galaxy, but I didn't see fibroids. I did spot a dolphin. "But they are harmless so we didn't remove them. Esther is fine and you can see her in a few minutes and she'll be ready to go home soon."

Soon? It was hours before I went to see her. A nurse led me past row after row of flimsy blue curtains until we got to Esther. She was sound asleep and hooked up to that machine that goes "ping". She was in a hospital gown and covered with a toilet-paper-thin sheet and a blanket only slightly thicker than my shirt. I knew she was cold. She's always cold.

She was fine, the procedure was textbook. But why did I cry while sitting there watching her? Maybe because she looked so helpless. Maybe because I felt so helpless and useless.

Esther calls me "Mr. Fix-it" when it comes to troubles – I don't want her to be sad or angry, I want to do something about it. Esther has taught me that sometimes I have to let things go their natural course. She's lying there and I can't help her. The doctors and nurses can help her, but I can't. I'm supposed to be her provider, her protector. Me big he-man, strong like bull.

Maybe I'm seeing the future. I'm sitting and watching her pass away. We did that with my mother back in 2001 – her cancer had metastasized and on her last day, a Saturday, Esther and I and my father sat by her bedside and watched her breathing get shallower and shallower until ten that evening.

Is it selfish of me to want to die first? I don't want to be without Esther. I was without her for 35 years and I don't want to be without her again.

But in a half-hour Esther awoke and asked for water. I filled a glass and helped her drink a little. She fell back asleep and I held her hand. A nurse walked in and said they were going to wake her up and dress her and I was to go back to the waiting area.

They wheeled her to my car. On the way from the parking lot I had to negotiate a stiff right turn and scraped my car on the faux-rock wall of the hospital. I still have the car and the scar on the back passenger side. The nurse and I helped Esther into the front seat. Esther slept through most of the drive through St. Louis and across the river to Illinois. She woke and asked if she could have a chocolate milk shake. We were very near the exit with a Jack-in-the-Box, which has the best shakes. I wasn't about to refuse her, and I was hungry, too. She didn't want anything to eat so I got a hamburger and drink for myself and a chocolate milk shake for her.

She took one drink and fell back asleep. A half-hour down the interstate I drank her shake. She didn't mind. At home I walked her to the bedroom where she slept most of the day.

She was all right.

And the fibroids had been banished back to the galaxy from which they came. Now it's into the Tardis and the hunt for our son or daughter. The worst was over, smooth sailing from here on, right?

⌒

*e*sther and her doctor had decided to try intrauterine insemination (IUI) before the more familiar in vitro fertilization (IVF). IUI sounds like those stories you hear on the news involving turkey basters. "Washed sperm" is injected into the uterus and everyone crosses their fingers and hopes one of the little swimmers fertilizes the egg. A washed sperm means that the sperm has been cleansed of any interfering goo it would otherwise have to swim through to get to the ovum. Less obstacles means more soldiers fighting their way into the egg and better chances that the one lucky guy makes it in and wins the race.

All right then, let's go!

Wait, I have to do what now?

I've had worse birthdays, but not many. When I was 29 turning 30 I started a weeks-long bout of flu, sinus infection and eventually pneumonia. I was in the midst of a trial when I felt that tell-tale tickle in the back of my throat indicating a cold was coming. By that evening, when a friend came by to take me out for dinner and drinking, the flu hit with all its fury and I was laid out on the couch for the rest of the weekend.

Now I was turning 39. Did we plan on going to my favorite restaurant? Then a nice bar for a few drinks? Then a movie or a concert? Finishing the day with a snuggle with the love of my life? No.

I had to go to the hospital to spew in a cup.

We spent the night before at the same Ramada Inn during our battle with the fibroids; ate at the same restaurant, read different books and watched different TV shows and then to bed. The next week Kevin Pollack was performing at the comedy club on the second floor of the hotel. Too bad, had I done this a week later I would have gone. I probably missed a great show.

Up and early to the hospital the next morning; my birthday. I filled out all the forms, gave them my insurance card and sat in a dark waiting area thumbing through Time magazine with the TV blaring CNN in the background. When my name was called I walked to the counter. They gave me a cup with a twist-on lid. This looked just like those cups I use when I have to give a urine sample. "I hope they don't expect the same volume," I said. "I hope they burn these cups when they're done with them. Is this a recycled one?"

"Write your name and birth date on the label, please," a nurse said. She walked me around the corner, past the nurse's station and into a small room. It was about the size of our bathroom at home except for a small bookcase next to the commode. A TV, a DVD player and a VCR set on top of the bookcase. There was a stack of dirty magazines in the corner.

"Feel free to take your time and look at the magazines and if you brought your favorite video tape or DVD there are the remotes," the nurse said.

I wasn't quite sure what she meant. "My favorite videotape? You mean, like Kelly's Heroes?"

Her eyebrows went up. "Well if that's what you like…"

Then I was quite sure what she meant. "Oh I see. Thanks."

She closed the door behind her and I never saw her again. Whereas, I have probably been the topic of many a conversation in her life ever since. "Yes, I've seen some weirdos in my day. There was one guy who got off watching Kelly's Heroes."

"Now dear," her husband says, men always standing up for one another during these sorts of things, "there's lots of machismo going on in that movie – Clint Eastwood, Telly Savalas, heck even Carroll O'Connor has a butch role. I get stiff just thinking about it. You can't help it! Lots of Y-chromosomes flying in that movie. Besides, Stuart Margolin is just so darn cute. So's Don Rickles, for that matter. Now Big Jake, THERE'S a movie loaded with testosterone…"

"Please dear, not during Christmas dinner…"

They took my donation and had it washed, cleaned and pressed. By now Esther and I waited in another room of the complex. She lay on a table with her legs splayed in stirrups and I sat beside her. She flinched a little when the doctor inserted the washed sperm, but otherwise she felt no pain. A little embarrassed to be sure, but no physical pain.

But then she had her period a few days later. The IUI didn't work.

We tried IUI again in May of 2004. That was quite a day, too. IUI in the morning and my sister's wedding in the afternoon.

It was back to the motel for the night before, back to the restaurant for dinner, and the next morning back to the hospital for another round. I found the same dirty magazine with exceptional pictorials of a lovely lady in compromising positions – her stretch marks and bullet scars expertly airbrushed out.

I wondered how they handled the donation cup. I wasn't allowed to bring any gloves or tongs (unless that was my turn on … and they mock my Kelly's Heroes fetish…). Did they use gloves? If I worked there I certainly would want to. Imagine going to medical school, residency, all those student loans and what do you do for a living?

Handle other men's spew.

There is only one other occupation in the world in which that is the main objective. Fortunately, the doctor is paid more than the prostitute. Sometimes. Depends on the prostitute. And the doctor. And the spew, for that matter.

Oh I suppose a motel maid and a janitor in a school gym sometimes encounter it, but I would consider that an occupational hazard as opposed to the main focus of the job.

We drove from St. Louis to Columbia, Illinois, where I lived in the early 1990s. We ate at a wonderful Thai restaurant for lunch then drove Route 3 to Route 13 to Carbondale where my sister married. I have three sisters – one was married in the late 1960s and I do not remember much of that. My younger sister (we are about 20 months apart) married in Carbondale too in the late 1980s. And now my youngest sissy in 2004. We went back home to Mount Vernon to complete the circle 24-hours later.

That IUI didn't take either. Was it the jostling of the long car ride? The stress (good stress) of the wedding? The Thai food?

We kept up the vitamins, the temperature-taking, the timing. And more IUIs.

We thought a lot about names during all this. We're not pregnant yet, but we wanted to establish a name. Some people wait until the baby is born – or even later – to pick a name. They want to see what kind of personality he or she has before deciding, I suppose.

I can respect that, but that's neither Esther's nor my style. We have to have a name. We're the type to have to know the sex of the baby, too. Not knowing if it is a boy or a girl until it was born would drive us crazy. It seems impractical nowadays to not know ahead of time. There is so much preparation and you can only take gender neutrality so far.

Names are very important. A name carries preconceived images. It can inspire awe or a giggle fit. Ever since Esther was a teenager she received letters asking her to join AARP – thinking she was an elderly woman.

Only four other Esthers come to mind when I think of the name – Esther Williams the swimmer. She made musicals in the 1940s. Those films that all had the same plot but spotlighted the beautiful-until-the-day-she-died Ginger Rogers dancing, or Sonya Henning ice skating or Esther Williams swimming. Caesar Romero played the love interest and Donald O'Conner was the comic relief – although he danced too – and danced very well.

There was the actress Esther Rolle from *Good Times* (wouldn't you love to have had her as your mother and John Amos as your father? They made a wonderful couple and had great chemistry).

Esther was the name of the grandmother from *The Waltons*. Then there was Aunt Esther from *Sanford & Son*, who … well, let's be frank; Redd Fox was right – could stick her face in dough and make gorilla cookies.

My name doesn't carry as much baggage as Esther's, but it has its quirks, too. There are as many ways to spell Michael as there are men named Michael. I've seen it all – Micheal, Michel, Michal, Mikel…

Plus there is the dichotomy of Michael and Mike. The names are complete opposites: Michael is elegant and noble. Saints and archangels are named Michael. Mike is earthy and curt (so is the name Curt, for that matter). Football coaches and tavern owners are called Mike.

Mike will argue with you; Michael will discuss the options with you. Mike listens to rock and roll; Michael listens to jazz and classical. Mike likes the Three Stooges; Michael does too – he's still a guy after all.

We didn't want a name with a lot of baggage. Neither were we going to pick a modern name that sounded like an adverb; very trendy among the Hollywood-starlet type. We weren't going to throw Boggle dice and use the letters that were rolled. Nor were we going to use the then-current trend of erratically-placed apostrophes, dashes, smiley-faces or elemental symbols in the name.

I did not want a name ending in "y". It would sound too much like he or she should be a Mouseketeer and, because of the last name, be cloying and sing-songy. In the 1980s I was enthralled with a girl named Candy. That was her real name, but I called her Candice. We talked briefly about marriage and I realized had we gotten married her name would have been Candy Curry. Candy Curry. Sounds like an Indian dessert, doesn't it?

Susy Curry, Jerry Curry, Mary Curry (my mother's name – she married into it and I doubt she was teased by her fellow classmates about it), Larry Curry, Brandy Curry. Neener-neener-nee-ner. No names ending in "y", please.

We wanted an older-sounding name. A classic. A name that brings up noble, olden days. "Well, how about Esther?" I said.

"No," said Esther. I don't blame her. Although I think it's a beautiful name.

My family is chocked full of old and little-used names. My aunts were named Iola, Marjory, Maxine, Iris, Genevieve, Annabelle and Donna. My father had aunts named Inez, Hazel and Lois; his mother was named Myrtle. But we agreed that if we were going to name the baby after a family member, it would be our parents, not great or great-great aunts.

Esther's parents' names are Harvey Eldon and Shirley Lucille. We didn't like any of those. My parents' names are Mary Alvenia and Kenneth Eugene. Mary? Mary Curry. Too sing-songy. Alvenia? No. Alvin, the male version? I went to high school with an Alvin, a wonderful guy who died in his forties. But no. No one will remember my high school friend; my son's school mates will only keep asking about Simon and Theodore. My father never liked the name Eugene – although my middle name is Gene – so that was out.

We liked Kenneth, so that went on the list. But I thought about combining the names into one. The odds are good this will be our only chance at a child (twins or not), so we'd best cram as many family names in as we could. Kenvenia? No. Mary-gene? Maryjean? Not bad. Pretty good, in fact.

Plus it harkens back to that great episode of *Mary Tyler Moore* when Georgette gave birth to her daughter in Mary's apartment. Since Mary and Lou Grant helped with the birth, she and her husband (Ted Baxter) decided to call the baby Marylou. "Sorry about giving you second billing, big guy," Ted told Lou, "but LouMary sounded dumb." Maryjean went on the list. I repeated the joke to my dad when we told him our final decision on the name ("Sorry about second billing Dad, but Kenvenia sounds dumb.").

Esther's parents' names made odd combinations too. Harley? No, they'll think he was named after the motorcycle. The only Harley I know was the legendary wrestler Harley Race. Naming him after wrestlers would certainly give him that machismo that comes with cool names.

Wouldn't you love to have one of those names that make women swoon just by saying it? You can be as ugly as an ape but you'd still have chicks crawling all over you if you tell them your name is Armand Assante. Antonio Banderras, Ricardo Montalban...

Harley Brisco – the middle name from another wrestler, Jack; not County Junior. My son, Harley Brisco Curry. "That's my son, the one standing on the other football player's head. His name's Harley, Harley Brisco. That was your son? Sorry about that. What's his name? Lester Kenvenia. Heh-heh. Yes, sorry…" And that certainly settled the naming business.

"No," said Esther.

Well, it was worth dreaming about.

Then how about Sheldon? That's pretty good too. That could be for a boy or a girl. Sheldon Leonard was the great actor and producer of "The Danny Thomas Show", "The Andy Griffith Show", its progeny, as well as one of the best TV shows ever made, "The Joey Bishop Show".

There was a great comic book artist Sheldon Meyer. Yeah, that works.

"Don't do it," said a female friend of Esther's named Shelley. "My full name is Sheldon and I always hated it. All through school they thought I was a boy and put me in the boy's gym class."

"Easily solved," I said, "her middle name will be Brisco and she can beat the hell out of all the boys!"

"No," said Esther, although Sheldon made the list for either boy or girl. Sheldon Maryjean Curry made it to the top of the list. All our parents names in one child.

Other names came up that we liked just as well. Evelyn was one. I liked Arwen – from the "Lord of the Rings". Just obscure enough that no one will pick on her (we wouldn't name a boy Frodo, for instance) but pretty. Esther didn't like it, though; she didn't like the actress from the movies. The decision on a name had to be unanimous, so Arwen was out. Eowyn and Galadriel weren't even considered.

In 2000 we honeymooned in Boston and visited President John Adams homestead and learned about Abigail Adams. I loved the character of Abigail Adams from one of my favorite movies "1776", played by the unbelievably beautiful Virginia Vestoff - with that long red hair and a singing voice that would knock you over. The one brief shot of her smiling in that movie still makes me swoon. The movie also starred Blythe Danner. If you are only going to have two women in a movie those would be my picks, too.

Abigail was also the name of the First Lady on *West Wing* – a TV show that was our favorite viewing at the time. Still is, actually – we still dig out the DVDs and watch the whole series in a marathon every few years.

Abigail Sheldon Curry. Or how about Abigail Maryjean Curry? We agreed. We had our girl name.

But what about a name for a boy?

Sheldon was still an option. William was also a strong possibility. William Sheldon Curry. William is a family name: Esther's brother was named William and so were my dad's brother, uncle and grandfather. William can also be shortened to Liam, as in Liam Neeson. We wouldn't be directly naming a son after the actor, but neither of us minded the connection. I don't think Liam Neeson has done a movie I do not like. At least I liked him in the movie even if the rest of it … well … sucks.

"Phantom Menace" comes to mind. Yippie…

A few years ago a childhood friend named his son William and now calls him Liam, but I don't think that is a big worry. Two friends naming their son the same name – eh. I doubt the kids will meet more than half-a-dozen times in their lives. Not a deal-breaker.

"How about Arthur," I asked Esther. Arthur is also a family name – Esther's brother-in-law and his son are named Arthur. Although we were looking for more unique names, having cousins with the same name is also not a problem. You can't throw a hard-boiled egg at my family reunion without hitting a Steve.

We had no problem naming a child after a male relative – uncles and brothers – but not female relatives. That doesn't seem fair, does it? I suppose it was because of the names. William and Arthur versus Hazel and Inez. Can you see the difference?

"That's a family name, sure. I like it," Esther said.

"Plus…." I said.

"Yes…?" Esther said, eyes narrowing.

Our son's name will be Arthur Curry. Do you know who Arthur Curry is? Arthur Curry is Aquaman's secret identity. Bruce Wayne is Batman, Clark Kent is Superman, Peter Parker is Spider-Man, Phyllis Diller is the Joker. Thus is Arthur Curry, Aquaman. Since childhood I've always loved the comic book character if only for that reason – the art and stories were pretty decent too. If we named a son Arthur, the nerds will love it and the bullies will have no idea and not pick on him (they'll find another reason I am sure…). I told Esther why I liked Arthur. The name Arwen I let die; but I would fight for Arthur…

"Okay," she said.

I was elated! Arthur Curry! How wonderful was that! And Arthur Sheldon Curry sounded good too! If my son wasn't going to be the *mas macho* Harley Brisco Curry, at least he can be Aquaman! We can decorate his room with pictures and drawings of the Monarch of the Deep – I still have my old 1970s Mego action figure we can put high high high out of reach on a shelf. His room will be painted to look like the briny deep – light and dark blues with bubbles, sea horses, sea weed...

"We can't do that," Esther said, "underwater scenes in a child's bedroom can lead to asthma."

What?

We'll use paint brushes, not rag weed. Nautical themes cause asthma? Really?

Do western themes cause a kid to be allergic to barbeque? Would a snowy/winter motif cause hyperthermia? Did Wes Craven have Munsch's "The Scream" painted over his bed? Okay, I won't argue, Esther is usually right about these things. "Can we put up a picture of Aquaman?"

"Oh sure." Thank God for that at least.

We have a boy's name and a girl's name. And if we have twins, imagine the fun I'll having singing their names to them. "Arthur and Abigail, Abigail and Arthur, Arthur and Abigail, Abigail and Arthur." And then it dawned in me ...

Our children's names will all start with the same initials.

Other than the SUV there is no greater signifier of yuppie fertility than children whose names all start with the same initials! I can't let that happen. I'll have to start playing golf and listening to U2. I'll have to download the latest TV reality show singalongs on i-tunes and have a cellular phone glued to my ear. We'll need to buy a Dodge Grand Caravan and some sort of canoe or other water craft. I'll have to start jogging and eating veggie pizza.

And I'll have to wear loafers. Loafers without socks. I'll be killing every flower I walk passed. And loose-fitting jeans. Or Dockers! And pastel shirts. Oh God in heaven, I can't wear pastel shirts, I'm too fat. I'll look like an Easter egg.

We'll have to go back to the mega-church in town. We just left the mega-church – because it was a mega-church! One of the drummers from the mega-church later visited our current church and asked Esther if they had met. "You stood next to her in the praise band every Sunday for three years," I said. That's how big it is!

We left and found a nice, friendly church that cares about the elderly and poor, but now we'll have to head back to the Superdome! Instead of looking at the minister we'll have to watch a big screen. Look! There we are! Wave! Wooo! And of course there's always someone with a "John 3:16" placard behind us. And we can't hear the sermon over the hawkers. "Programs! Gitcher programs! You won't know what verse to turn to without a program!" "Wine! Sacramental wine!" "Host! I got fresh host right here! Who wants to do this in remembrance of our Lord?"

And the music! No hymns, just rock and roll with the word "Jesus" substituted for the word "baby". "Jesus, Jesus hold me tight; Jesus, Jesus all through the night." "Falling for you Jesus, falling for you bad."

Oh how I long for the days as a kid sitting in an un-air-conditioned Presbyterian church moaning a dirge about being joyful. And singing it after spending 45 minutes hearing an examination of the third chapter of Jonah. If that sort of church experience is good enough for me, it's good enough for Arthur and Abigail. Damn kids.

But Abigail and Arthur are such cute names. And they'll be cute babies. And I already love them. And if starting their names with the same initials means I'll have to join in the lifestyle I have spent my adulthood mocking then so be it. I am a father. I'll do it.

"Did you say something?" Esther asked.

"No," I said.

So the names were settled.

Unless we had two boys. Or two girls. What then?

The two girl names were settled quickly: Abigail Sheldon and ... Something Maryjean. Esther had nixed Evelyn by this time and we were struggling to find another name for a second girl.

I already feel sorry for them when it's time to learn to spell their names, but there are no apostrophes or ellipses or emoticons so they won't have it as bad as some of their classmates.

We went back over our list of boys names. Arthur Sheldon, check. William Kenneth? Neh. Kenneth William? Again, neh. Besides, naming one son after his grandfather would leave the other grandfather out. We can't honor one without honoring the other. But William can stay.

William ... William what?

"Michael," said Esther.

"Yes," wondering what I had done wrong that she had to use my full name.

"No, William Michael; that would be a nice name, William Michael Curry."

"Michael? Me? You'd let us name a son after me?"

"Yes, of course."

My lower lip started to wobble. My son would have my name. Who wouldn't be happy about that? Oh sure I've groused in the past about clients who are Seniors or Juniors or "the Third". "Now be sure to put Junior on there, otherwise people will think it's my father."

I have to do extra work because your father was too dumb to think of another name. Isn't that a treat for me? Of course naming my son after me is completely different – hey, it's my double standard...

And we're talking about the middle name – completely different. Middle names have no purpose other than giving a parent someone else to yell at when you are REALLY in trouble. If I was playing outside and my mother yelled my name to come in ("Michael!"), I knew I still had a few minutes. If she used the middle name ("Michael Gene!"), I had scant seconds to beat feet to the back door. More likely it was already too late and I was in trouble for staying outside.

Plus a middle name, a good middle name, provides an overall balance between the first and last name. The full name has to flow, all while addressing the potential good and bad aspects of the individual names. Arthur Sheldon Curry could be a law professor. Harley Brisco Curry would be an all-college pro. Arthur Brisco Curry would be a rodeo clown ... and his initials would be ABC. No, I couldn't do that to my son. Harley Sheldon Curry? It has a nice flow but a closer hearing reveals its flaws. The images don't fit: the tough Harley and the softer Sheldon.

Well, it made sense to me at the time. If there is anyone out there named Harley Sheldon I would love to talk to you someday about your name and how it affected your life, your lifestyle, your career. Maybe I made a horrible mistake by throwing out Harley Sheldon as a name. Then again, maybe after our meeting I will be glad I dodged that bullet. I won't say that in front of you, though, I promise. I'm not cruel.

⟶

*W*e decided for the big swing, the long ball, the Hail Mary. Yes, I'm mixing my sports metaphors, sorry about that – but those aren't really my forte. This is a guy thinking about naming his son after Aquaman – you think I'd be able to get a sports metaphor correct?

It was time to consider In Vitro Fertilization: IVF. The treatment everyone knows about and reads about. Esther takes shots and meds to create lots of eggs and the sperm is injected into each one. Three or four fertilize and are placed inside Esther where they will hopefully stay and grow into a litter of kids.

To this day I feel awful about having to put Esther through such an ordeal. I couldn't give her the shots so she had to do it herself. I hope I was otherwise supportive. I hope she thinks I was supportive – except for the shots. I couldn't bring myself to inject needles into her. I just couldn't do it. I'm sorry my dearest love...

This time we went to another hospital in St. Louis – near the previous one but south a few miles. The previous hospital was private and Catholic and they are somewhat squeamish about the whole ... well ... watch Monty Python's Meaning of Life.

The doctor harvested seven eggs and I again donated my manliness. We took Esther home and waited for the results. This was two weeks before Christmas. We decided not to go to my office Christmas party; if only because of the stress of the IVF and the uncomfortable, if well-meaning, questions that would be asked. Instead that Friday and Saturday we went to St. Louis, ate a wonderful meal, watched a movie and spent the night in a nice hotel – we made it a lovely mini-vacation and date night.

I had never missed an office Christmas party. Everyone dressed nicely; we had a wonderful meal, a cash bar and a present exchange. It was one of those exchanges that, if it was your turn, you could "steal" a previously opened present and the victim could either steal another gift or open a new present.

This is fun for about eight to ten people. Thirty-two? Not so much fun. Quite boring actually – especially when three people constantly fight over the same gift and I am sitting holding a tin of stale cookies. But sometimes the presents were worth the fight – the owner always brought some deer sausage and cheese that caused quite a few battles. One year it was a fight over "Far Side" calendars. Someone once brought a DVD set of old cheesy science fiction movies. Another year - a rubber chicken that squawked when you squeezed it. I didn't get the movies, and never won the deer sausage basket; but I did get the rubber chicken. Oh God how our cats HATE that chicken! Bwah-hah-hah! Well, no bother, I would have plenty of years to attend Christmas parties – this was one of our last chances at having children – I was glad to miss the party if it meant starting our family.

None of the eggs took. That is to say not one of the eggs harvested and inseminated were viable. Not a one. Two had been fertilized, but they would not develop properly. It was doubtful the fertilized eggs would last more than a week or so even if they did implant themselves.

What could be the problem here?

We already examined Esther's plumbing; it was my turn.

I had to donate yet again. This wasn't 100 miles away in St. Louis but at my local hospital. I was given another cup and led to the bathroom in the middle of the nurse's station. No TV, no DVD player, no magazines, no gloves or tongs.

Just lots of distractions – phones rang; nurses walked past the bathroom door and were at their stations talking about who-knows-what. Except for one lady – she made it very clear she wanted to order lunch.

That was the last straw. She was coaxing the others to decide what to do for lunch. It was going on eleven o'clock and if they were going to order something it would have to be soon. "Does anyone want to get a pizza? Let's get a pizza."

"What kind of pizza does everybody want?" she said again, "I want a pepperoni pizza."

I opened the bathroom door. "Do. You. MIND? I am trying to masturbate!"

No, I didn't open the door and shout that; but I wanted to. If I did they would be staring at me when I finally left. I thought it best to be anonymous about the whole ordeal. Besides, I've given enough nurses stories to tell through the generations. "You wouldn't believe what some guy shouted a few years back." "That's nothing, let me tell you about the Kelly's Heroes guy…"

The doctor said it was low sperm count and motility problems. Back to a military analogy – I was the US Army in 1860 or 1937. I wasn't fighting with a full battalion and my soldiers were old and tired. All right then, how do I increase my recruitment? Diet? Do I need to add more almonds and blueberries to my snacks? Add more time on the treadmill? Less? Oh wouldn't that be nice… Start wearing boxers? I would hate that – I'm (con)strictly a brief man…

They wanted to take some x-rays to make sure there wasn't something else going on. So back to the hospital where another nurse had me drop trou while she pointed a huge humming machine at my crotch and told me to relax while she dove behind a lead wall.

Trying to drown out the metallic grinding noise of the X-ray machine, I thought to myself, "I'll bet this is how some superhero in the comic books got his powers." Pelted with mysterious X-rays, humble Michael Curry became endowed with powers and abilities far beyond those of mortal men. By day an attorney, at night he becomes … X-ray Crotch Man! I could join the Avengers – anyone can join the Avengers. The Justice League of America is harder to join – Wonder Woman blackballs everybody…

When it was all done she walked me to the exit. She took me by the arm while we walked. I thought that was very kind of her. Later I wondered if she pitied me.

I had some blockage in my passageways. Not enough to be dangerous, but enough to affect the sperm getting through. Clearing this up would help my sperm count and their motility. The more unwearied the soldiers, the better chance the fertilized eggs would develop and grow. Then the IVF would "take". I didn't like the idea of surgery, but if Esther could do it to fight off the villainous fibroids, I can get roto-rooted.

Some weeks later I went back to the hospital in St. Louis for my pre-operation work. I sat in a small room where I was poked, pricked, prodded, injected, inspected, detected, infected, neglected and selected by an otherwise friendly nurse. In the course of the 12-point inspection she said, "Your blood sugar is very high."

"Oh," I said.

"We can't do the operation while your blood sugar is this high."

"No?" I said. She couldn't explain to my satisfaction why not (of course to be fair, I was not in a very understanding mood) – an operation is an operation. If I had appendicitis or were in a car crash and needed surgery I doubt the doctor would shout out, "Hold on! This guy's blood sugar is too high, nothing we can do! Call the widow – er – the wife!"

But Nurse Ratchet was unmovable. So, I have to lower my blood sugar to have the operation to clear out the sperm tunnels to allow more active sperm to end up in the cup to be washed and inseminated into my wife so that we may have a litter of kids. OK, fine. I'll do it.

Esther's blood doctor is near Carbondale, a university town in southern Illinois. We made an appointment with him and I was again poked, pricked and prodded.

I had diabetes. All those years of savoring M&Ms had come home to roost.

I don't do shots; I cannot do shots. I couldn't give Esther her shots and I certainly wasn't going to give myself shots.

Fortunately, my new doctor said, my diabetes could be controlled with pills.

Pills? Pills I can do. As long as there are no shots involved, I could take enough pills to choke Elvis.

And I was given enough pills to do just that. Metformin and Glipizide for the blood sugar, but those would raise my cholesterol; so another prescription to lower my cholesterol. Plus an aspirin regimen to thin the blood – blood clots may become an issue. Plus, I still took the vitamins and supplements from the beginning of this quest.

Then came the diet. My beloved M&Ms were out. So were raisins. We cut back on anything with enriched flour (white bread). This I didn't mind. I like my bread dark. Really dark. So dark it absorbs the light from the refrigerator (and I always keep bread in the refrigerator...). But even then very little bread. I can still eat my fish and chicken slathered in hot sauce – just not as a sandwich. I can accept that.

Most pasta was out – spaghetti, ziti, lo mein, SpaghettiOs.

No. Absolutely not. I may go blind, I may lose all feeling in my feet, the hair may drop off my legs, but I will not abandon that neat round spaghetti you can eat with a spoon. I will not let go of my childhood friend. I ate a can a day as a youngster; well, it seemed like it.

We compromised and allowed SpaghettiOs in moderation – and I would eat the kind with meatballs or franks for the protein. As I understand it, the protein counters the starch. Hey, I may be wrong, I'm a lawyer not a doctor, and my world had turned upside down; cut me some slack…

So O's once every few weeks as a snack. Weeks later I realized I had not eaten any at all. If they had not mentioned pasta, I probably would not have noticed I hardly ate O's anymore. I guess it was the principle – wanting to have some kind of control or to be able to rebel at some part of this process.

Peanut butter was okay (in moderation) and nuts were fine, too.

I went to a free dietary class for diabetics at the hospital. Unfortunately I was the only one there. Ick, I was hoping to be a face in the crowd; now I am in for a one-on-one conversation. The fellow who taught the class was very nice and had plenty of visual aids – lots of plastic food. We discussed what was good to eat – "vegetables are free,' he said.

"Tell that to the security guard at the grocery store," said I.

"No, that means you can eat as many vegetables as you want…" said he.

"Ah!" said I. "That's great! I could eat potatoes and corn all day!"

"…except potatoes and corn," said he.

He meant green vegetables – broccoli, Brussels sprouts, celery. Well, all right – I can eat those, too. That's why God made Velveeta, butter and peanut butter respectively…

I realized later I was missing the point of all this.

He brought out a brown rectangular piece of plastic and put it on the table in front of me. "This is one serving of meat. It's about the size of a deck of cards."

A serving of meat? That's a serving of meat? That's a forkful of meat. I find bigger pieces of meat when I floss.

When these damn kids are born they will be grounded until they're twenty-five!

I also got back on the treadmill. I had been using it off and on for years but I was determined to exhaust and sweat down my blood sugar. I hated it. I much prefer a brisk walk outside, but I would only have a short amount of time to walk in the evenings when I get home before bed. Plus I am not an outdoor guy. There is about a two-week window in the spring and fall when the weather is neither too hot nor too cold to run outside. And it would be embarrassing and humiliating, let's be honest. I'm not exactly the athletic type. Neighbors would see me out there and laugh. I should know – I laugh at them. Old men would pass me, so would children on tricycles. No, best to keep my dignity by staying inside.

I got up a half-hour earlier in the morning to go to the basement and "tread", then shower and off to work. My cousin (an avid runner) suggested I watch TV or listen to music I enjoy to make the treading more enjoyable. So I listened to CDs of old radio shows (Fibber McGee & Molly and Jack Benny were faves, as was the Shadow), Van Morrison's "Moondance", "The Last Waltz" by the Band, the Moody Blues, the Beatles, anything.

It did the trick – running in place while chanting the "na-nas" of Caravan, munching rabbit food, nibbling on the one serving of meat dangling off my fork and taking so many pills Judy Garland would be jealous – and my blood sugar was down from the six hundreds to double digits

Back to the hospital in St. Louis for my second pre-operation check.

The drive to St. Louis is long but fruitful. I always stop at my favorite book stores and hobby shops/game shops. "BC" – when fun money was plentiful.

I announced my arrival at the check-in booth and signed my name. A hand-written note on the window caught my eye, and I told the receptionist I would be right back.

Cell phones are the tool of the devil. I don't besmirch anyone who has one permanently glued to their ear (so it seems), but it's not for me. I dislike talking on the telephone anyway, but now with cell phones I can dislike talking on the phone anywhere I like – at a restaurant, in the car, sitting quietly in the park. I bristle when I am talking to someone and they shut me up to answer their phone. "Excuse me," they imply, "whoever this is, they are MUCH more important than talking to you right now." Look at those rows of teenagers texting on their phones – probably to someone standing right next to them. Zombie apocalypse indeed.

But Esther worried about me when I was on the road so she got me a cell phone for emergencies. It is a very simple phone (it has a rotary dial) compared to hers – she has a phone that can do a thousand things. A thousand and one if she actually uses it as a phone. I keep mine in the glove box of my car and use it when I need to call work or call Esther to tell her I am on my way home.

After reading the note at the hospital I had to go get my cell phone and called Esther from the waiting room. "Sweetie? There is a sign on the window here at the hospital. As of Friday they will stop accepting my insurance."

The state of Illinois could force insurance companies to pay for infertility treatments, but they couldn't force medical providers from accepting every insurance company. What was the point of going through a pre-operation check today if I can't afford the operation next week? I didn't think about asking if they could rush the operation before the cut-off; but I doubt that would have been possible.

Oh we had enough disposable income to pick up a book or two at Borders, but not enough to pay for an operation.

I asked Esther if I should just head home. She said yes.

⌒

There was not one particular thing that was causing our infertility. The fibroids caused a problem, but they were removed. By now Esther was 40 and her eggs were getting old. So were my sperm. Cleaning out the pipes might increase motility, but even then there was no guarantee.

By now Esther was offered the job of Assistant Head Librarian. This was the number two spot and carried with it more responsibility and more income. But she needed a master's degree to get the job. They went through the formalities of an interview and also took other applications, but they wanted Esther to get the job and got it she did. But she had to get that degree.

There was no place locally she could get her master's degree. The nearest universities that offered it were still a hundred miles away. She looked into online courses, but even they had occasional face-to-face classes. The best places to get a Masters in Library Science (or Library Science and Information Technology) both online and nearby were the University of Illinois in Champaign and the University of Missouri-Rolla. The UM face-to-face classes met in St. Louis at the UMSL campus. This was a much shorter drive than Champaign.

There was a problem with her degree from the Christian college. She already had a Masters but the curriculum didn't jibe with what Mizzou required.

There was also her GPA. At her previous school they were draconian about grading – their scale was much higher than other schools – a B there would be an A- anywhere else.

She had to take the MSAT again; including its math section. Esther doesn't like math and wasn't very good at it. After much studying, though, she passed!

She applied for and was accepted at Mizzou. A big 12 school! Boola-boola! I know that's Yale; don't criticize, celebrate with us!

An energetic twenty-something might be able to juggle work, school and a newborn. But twins? Triplets? A purple heart to anyone who has; but Esther and I decided that would be too much for us. Had we plenty of grandparents, sibling and friends who could take turns watching the kids, maybe. Maybe. But we didn't.

So until the insurance thing got realigned, we decided to put any further IFVs and IUIs on hold while Esther concentrated on her degree. This was in 2005.

Which turned into 2006, then 2007, then 2008…

Two

ADOPTION

Why did we decide to adopt? By 2009 any infertility treatments, if we could find a hospital that would take my insurance, would be less and less likely to succeed because of our age. I was 44; Esther, 43. We were both practical enough to realize getting pregnant would be tough. Not impossible, but very tough. Would I be able to muster the encouragement for Esther to help her go through all the shots and stirrups she went through half a decade ago?

Plus she said from the beginning she would be willing to go through this until she turned 40. That was her deadline. The IVF/vacation-for-ourselves-let's-miss-the-office-Christmas-party was in November 2004; a month later she was 39. Her deadline passed the next year.

Now it was New Years Day 2009 and I was packing away the Christmas decorations and presents. I looked one last time at the Christmas cards taped to our mantel and spotted one from an old friend with his wife and children. It wasn't a Christmas-y or wintery photo. I think they were standing in short sleeves in front of a fountain. But they were smiling – a smile that reached their eyes. It was a smile that showed peace and love: real, familial, inner peace and love. Not that my life with Esther was not peaceful or loving; I loved and still love her more and more every day. But ours was a love times two. Not three or four or more. Their smiles rekindled my feelings of wanting a family that had died out over the past five years.

Fertilization treatments are out, what about adopting?

What would it take to adopt? I spent most of that New Year's Day (Thursday) and Friday searching the internet for information. I read through all the horror stories and gushing testimonials. I readied my presentation to Esther. I didn't expect her to reject the idea – I just knew she would have lots of questions and I didn't want to sound like this was a flighty whim. Creating and designing my own board game – THAT was a whim. This was not.

Was time running out for adopting? We were getting older and although I did not find anything on age limitations I knew it would be harder for us if we waited. We might be limited as to the age of the child. Although adopting an older child – even a teenager – would have been just as wonderful, I did not want to limit our options.

By now Esther's post-graduate schooling was going full bore and she had two years to go – and making straight "A"s by the way! Some classes were tremendously hard, some ridiculously easy. For example, each week her assignment in her children's literature class went something like this: "This week I have to tape and critique a children's show." "This week I will have to read a comic book."

I led her to the rows and rows of boxes in the side room where I kept my comic books. "Here, take your pick!"

She decided on a comic aimed at children. She picked a Hardy Boys manga book from the library; but she appreciated my help.

So the problems with having and rearing a child while attending school were diminishing while the problems with having and rearing a child because of our age were increasing. If we were going to look seriously at this thing, we better do it now while we were between the crashing waves.

Type "adoption" into your favorite browser and you will get the same feeling of overwhelming nausea I had that New Year's Day. But just like any road map you take it one little line to another little line and the pieces start to fit. Thin black line to thick blue line, sometimes a thick green line will get you there faster, but it's a toll road. Avoid the grey lines. Eventually, you will find the best way to your destination.

Our destination on the afternoon of Saturday, January 3rd *anno domini* 2009 was 9th Street Grill.

We live in Mount Vernon, near the center of southern Illinois. It is 75 miles from the Mississippi River and the city of St. Louis. It is about 60 miles from Carbondale, Illinois; home of Southern Illinois University and about the same miles to Evansville, Indiana. Springfield, Indianapolis, Paducah and other cities are too far for less than an all-day jaunt. That means if you want to dine on something different, see a play or exhibit or, for that matter, a non-blockbuster film, you have to plan for a long drive and probably an overnight stay.

It is a town where two interstates meet; a good place to stop and stretch your legs or stay overnight on your way to someplace else. If you want to gas up the car and get some fast food or sit and eat at a chain restaurant, this is the place. I think it's the perfect place for bus tours to stop – far away enough from a city to not be hectic, but big enough you can find something to do in the evenings other than watch the interstate traffic go by.

Mount Vernon has some good restaurants and a nice multiplex; although clothing stores, book stores and the like are fading away as they are in most towns. We have lots of chain restaurants, too. Nothing wrong with that – if you like their menus.

Esther and I have two restaurants we like to frequent. Both have excellent food and excellent service and are as different as can be.

One is Silver Streak, east of town across the railroad tracks. Once located in a train depot, it was a bar that served food. At the turn of the millennium they moved across the street and became a restaurant that served liquor. They serve good steak and tilapia, but I go there for the hamburgers, jalapeño poppers and their chicken salad. Ah, the chicken salad. The best anywhere. I prefer to put extra mayo on my chicken salad – I prefer it more soupy than dry. Either way their chicken salad is to me what Adam's Ribs cole slaw was to Hawkeye Pierce on "MASH".

Their specials were also tasty – meatloaf, shepherd's pie, fried chicken. I don't remember what they called it, but about once a year they made a salad with pepperoni, strawberries and poppy seed dressing. Oh, mommy…

It was the place we went to after church. We took our families there when they were driving through town, or to give them a good send-off before they hit the road. Esther and her librarian co-workers (now employees) went there every day for lunch to have a sandwich or a seafood chef salad.

What would be the collective noun for librarians? When you see two or more librarians together, what would you call them? A group? A herd? I've decided to call them a "shush". A shush of librarians ate lunch at Silver Streak. Has a nice ring and it makes sense. More so than a sleuth of bears at any rate...

The other restaurant is 9th Street Grill. It opened in 2007 and Esther and I have been regulars ever since. It is the yin to Silver Streak's yang. Silver Streak serves great strawberry pie; 9th Street has crème brulee. Peanut butter pie versus la Femme Volant.

9th Street does steaks, seafood and pasta served in many a strange way: peppered, Cajun, curried. It is probably the only place in an 80-mile radius one can get soups like gazpacho and spicy peanut. Their mulligatawny was so good Esther looked up the recipe to make her own.

It is the place to take your boss for lunch (or have him take you if he has bad news). We would go every Saturday afternoon or evening. We always knew when some school had prom or homecoming – teens in tuxes and (sometimes inappropriate) dresses came and went all evening.

Being regulars is embarrassing sometimes – waiters and waitresses could tell Esther what she was going to order as we sat. I guess it is classier than "the usual?" It got to the point we expected them to have it already prepared as we walked in.

The salmon, regular not spicy, red-skin potatoes, ranch on the salad with no onions. Hey, if something is good, don't mess with it.

I always threw them curveballs, though. I changed my order depending on my mood. At first it was the calzone with anchovies, tomatoes and onions. No, seriously. Then they added sausage and pepperoni to their pizza/calzone menu. So it was a calzone with sausage, pepperoni and bacon. Then I discovered the Gambit –a pasta dish with sausage, shrimp and chicken in a hot sauce. Sometimes very hot! Depending on the soup, I would have soup instead of salad.

Occasionally their specials were too good to resist – curry chicken or shrimp (hey, if they were going to name it after me the least I could do was order it), lobster ravioli, etc.

They also serve a hummus tray as an appetizer.

I discovered the joy of hummus at Saleem's, a restaurant in University City in St. Louis. "Where garlic is king," its motto says, "and Allah is God," I added. Before moving to Mount Vernon it was my favorite place to go with my friends. I don't remember the chicken dish I ordered there, but it was tasty and garlicky. After the hummus appetizer, the chicken entrée, a few beers and some Turkish coffee for a closer, we left full, satisfied and ready for the rest of the evening.

I took Esther to Saleem's a few times before and after we married. She fell in love with the hummus too.

When we saw it as an appetizer on the 9th Street Grill menu we jumped for joy; figuratively of course - the people at the table next to us might not appreciate our bounding about. "What did they order," they would ask the waitress.

"The hummus."

"What's in it?"

"Crushed chick peas, garlic, lemon juice…"

"Is it worth leaping around our table for?"

"They seem to think so…"

9th Street Grill is the only restaurant around that serves hummus. The local grocery chain used to sell dusty cans of it, but … that was in a can for heaven's sake. This stuff is fresh and had nice crunchy veggies and pita bread to dip. Ah the joys of brushing the heaping pile of hummus with a bit of broccoli; or stabbing the hummus with a carrot stick, twisting it to get as much hummus as I could before savoring its flavor.

As Abby got older we stopped ordering it. Appetizers and toddlers do not mix. By the time the appetizer was done, so was she. Before we received our entrées Abigail was ready to go home. Never a pretty sight.

Two different restaurants; two different atmospheres and each excellent in their own way. How wonderful is that?

⌒

Late afternoon of January 3, 2009; the hostess at 9th Street took us to an open table – first one from the entrance on the south wall.

Esther ordered her usual. I don't remember what I ordered but it was probably the Gambit or a calzone. And the hummus platter.

"I have an important question to ask you," I said. I have only said this to Esther two or three other times in our relationship. One I remember vividly: it was when I proposed.

"Okay," Esther said. She knew I would not turn this into a silly joke or routine, and gave me her whole attention.

"Would you like to think about adopting a baby?"

"I would like that," she said.

Much like a previous "important question" - my proposal – it was vague. She still laughs about the way I proposed: "maybe in a few years if we are still together and you have not ripped my eyes out we can get married."

I proposed on January 1, 2000. What is it about early January that brings out the serious questions?

I made it into a joke in case she said "no", so we could laugh about it and I could save face. But she said she would marry me. We shortened the engagement by several years to the fall of 2000.

Now I asked another vague but important question to give her a chance to say "no" without making me feel foolish. Not "would you like to adopt a child", but "would you like to think about adopting a child."

"Oh we can think about it," she might say, "I can also think about stabbing you in the neck with this fork, but I'm not going to actually do it."

But she said yes. Again! Well, this yes was cautious. As with the marriage proposal, we stripped away the vagueness and evasion down to a simple "wanna adopt?" "Yes."

It was a bombshell, I admit; an ambush. I kept my research from the previous two nights to myself (she had even walked behind my chair while I was looking at adoption websites without so much as a "what are you looking at?") and I gave no hint what I was about to ask.

She answered quickly. Very quickly. She later said she had also been thinking about adoption. There we go again – thinking the same thoughts. I might have known…

I was exhausted that afternoon. I had tossed and turned the night before thinking and deciding about adoption.

Through the meal we discussed what I had found on the net. After dinner we got dessert at the Dairy Queen (Blizzards for us both: Snickers for her, M&Ms for me – yes I was still taking the diabetes pills but it's Dairy Queen, cut me some slack), went home and browsed the websites I had bookmarked.

We discussed adoption during the fertilization treatments, but we were scared off by all the bad scenarios that make up a good percentage of Lifetime's Movies of the Week;

Knock knock, "Hi, I'm the birthmother and I'm now 18 and off crack and I want my baby back. Here's a lawyer that will bankrupt you if you don't hand it over now."

Knock knock. "Hi, I'm the baby's natural father and I initialed where I should have signed so the entire adoption is invalid. Officer, go get the baby."

Knock knock, "Hi, were from the government. China wants their baby girls back. Where is the little darling'?" (Esther was especially concerned about this one.)

Knock knock. "Hi, we're the natural grandparents and since the real mother was a minor, we..." You get the idea.

The rest of the weekend we dug further into the internet. Esther ordered books from the library.

First we looked at international adoptions.

Spending too much time away from home was a primary factor. Adopting from Kazakhstan seemed streamlined but it required us to live there for seven weeks! Seven weeks!? On top of the few weeks here to bond with the child? We wouldn't have jobs at the end of that time period!

Korea brought their children to the US – all that was required was a trip to the west coast to pick him or her up, so that had potential.

China has now added health restrictions to adoptions - and both Esther and I would probably be over their required maximum body mass index.

Romania, that mecca of adopting parents from years past, is now closed to international adoptions. Why? When they blocked adoptions in 2004, Alin Teodorescu, head of the Chancellery for the Prime Minister of Romania said, "we are stopping corruption in the child-care system and trying to rebuild the whole system as a modern one." I'm from Illinois, why is one exclusive from the other? Best not to stick my nose in their business...

On a whim I checked Ireland and England. Can we adopt from there? No. If the child is a blood relative and he or she is otherwise orphaned, you might have a chance, but most "first world" countries were out.

As I write this (the mid 2010s), most countries have restricted US adoptions. As countries do better economically and start to gain a sense of national pride, they are less inclined to give Americans their babies.

But that was five years in the future, as it stood in the first days of 2009, if time and travel are a primary concern, our choices seem to be the Pacific Rim, South America and Africa.

So which should it be? Should that even be a consideration? Although I feel beastly saying so and I sound like a bigot, I did not want to raise an African child here. Esther agreed. The town I live in (or in which I live ... darn preposition stranding ...) has a strong African-American population; but it also has a strong ... mmm ... anti-African-American population. People have been known to use certain antebellum ethnic slurs even in front of strangers without considering how completely offensive they are. In the 1990s, when I had staff members with teenage children, the schools would close early at times because of ... well, in my day they would have called them race riots. Nowadays I suppose some sociologist has come up with some multi-syllabic nonsense that softened the words' impact – inter-ethnical physical conflict, or some such.

We might get around that with the private schools in the area, but eventually, unavoidably, someone will use the N-word to insult my child and then (let's be honest) his or her adoptive father (me) would then be on death row, perpetuating the stereotype.

There is a small Asian community in and around the town though (I guess local bigots are only taught to hate and fear black people. I'm sure Asians face bigotry in other areas of the country...), so that was less of a concern. We also agreed that an Hispanic child could be raised here with little problems (we live nowhere near Lou Dobbs).

⟨⟶

*O*nline we found a lot of Christian-based adoption agencies focusing on American children. We were not specifically looking for Christian-based agencies; they just seemed predominant on the search engines. A musician named Steven Curtis Chapman is more or less the guru of adoption in Contemporary Christian Music circles, His name and quotes from his songs pop up a lot on various websites. Esther knows who he is and listens to his music; I don't. He doesn't sing the modern-style "Love me, Jesus, do me all night long..." type of songs I complained about before, but it's still not my thing. I'd rather hear a Moody Blues CD...

A website I shared with Esther that first evening was the Adoption Network Law Center out of California. Like most businesses it had mixed reviews. Usually someone doesn't write a review if they are pleased, only if they are angry and want to "get back" at the company. I've done it and it's been done to me.

The bulk of its complaints were about the expense and the lack of contact with the staff. Plus it got mired in the "agency versus facilitator" argument.

To this day I don't know whether to call it an agency, a law firm or a facilitator.

What is the difference between an agency and a facilitator? It depends on who you ask and whose side you are on, if the internet definitions are any indication. Facilitators are either unlicensed, non-regulated, out-of-control baby brokers who may or may not take your money and disappear into the Ethernet. An agency is a clean, wholesome and licensed place whose staffs are trained professionals and hold themselves accountable for their actions under any circumstances. OR, a facilitator is a company that offers comfortable and person-to-person advice and counsel to help you choose among their many and various options when it comes to adoption; as opposed to a government-run-agency-out-of-Ayn-Rand's-worst-nightmares that will strangle you and the child with its red tape - by the time you adopt the child you will also be able to adopt his or her grandchildren.

The main difference is cost: an agency (if you ask a facilitator) or a facilitator (if you ask an agency), will dizzy you with their legal wrangling and drown you in so much fees and costs you will file bankruptcy within a year.

Oddly enough this is very reminiscent of the difference between bankruptcy attorneys and petition preparers.

I expected a good agency/facilitator would combine the best and worst – a reputable business offering personal communication while still supplying snarling red tape at crippling costs. This fit the bill.

It's not an insult – costs and red tape are expected. We chose that firm, hoped for the best and prepared for the worst.

Esther made one demand when we decided on the firm. "Would you take care of the phone calls and the paperwork?"

"Of course," I said. She had done most of the work – including the physical stress and strain – during our infertility treatments. She probably did not want to go through all that again just to be disappointed. Again. Plus she had her school and the new position at her job taking a lot of her time.

I called the firm on Monday the fifth. I provided some basic information – our names, addresses, ages, where we worked, and our interests - and scheduled a full-fledged phone interview for that Thursday evening. Three days later, Esther and I huddled in front of the speaker phone and called the 800-number.

The caseworker for that first interview was Marta. We discussed our personal information, as I had done that Monday. She told us how her firm did what it did. Basically, a birthmother who is giving her yet-to-be-born baby for adoption picks potential families from one of three Facebook-style web pages. We meet the birthmother and if we are all agreeable that a "match" is made, all the paperwork is prepared and filed with the appropriate state. When the baby is born we pick him or her up from the hospital that day and presto! Easy as pie!

Simple, right?

Ha!

Marta also answered questions about the financing and the procedures we have to go through. She did a very good job of assuaging our fears.

She told us that adopting nationally and internationally cost about the same, although the expenses were different. One is not more difficult than the other. I realize I was asking an encyclopedia salesman if I needed encyclopedias, but I found her reasoning logical and assuring. She said the same things as the books and websites I read.

Esther and I convinced ourselves that the *knock-knock* scenarios we feared were extreme and not the norm. Marta assured me that was correct - they are quite rare. I asked her, "Is it kind of like: look at all the airline flights from New York to North Carolina that didn't crash in the Hudson River and never made the nightly news?" "Yes, exactly."

We talked about our goals. At first I thought that was kind of silly – our goal is pretty obvious really – the counter worker at McDonald's rarely asks, "so what bring you here?" "Food."

We discussed our wants and needs. We talked about our nationality preference and our fear of raising an African-American child in a potentially hostile environment – mentally, not physically. Since they deal mainly in newborns, we did not discuss whether we would like to adopt an older child.

We agreed that a "package" would be fine. If the birthmother had older children would we be interested in adopting the family? Yes we would. A newborn plus a three or four-year old (or even older) brother or sister is a possibility. I would hate to have a family split up.

Marta also went through a long list of ailments and handicaps. We didn't care if the baby was born blind or deaf. Glasses or braces? Didn't care (if we had a child naturally, it would need glasses as both of us wear them; my lenses are thicker than most car windshields). Club foot, diabetes, correctable handicaps? No problems. As Esther said, "they're correctable."

The only things we said "no" to were severe autism, palsy or Down's Syndrome. It would not be fair to raise a child and then he or she be "orphaned" again when we die. Who would take care of him or her? It's certainly not fair to the (then grown) child or to whoever has to care for him when we're gone. He or she would have no siblings to help him when we die. No nearby family either. He would have to go to Assisted Living. Neither Esther nor I would do that to our child.

I was afraid that sounded selfish of us. "Oh you can't be bothered with a medically troubled child; you just want your precious little accessory you can show at parties."

Marta, and later our family and friends, said that was not selfish. Quite the contrary. She also said we did not look like bigots for not wanting to raise a black child in our town. A friend told me "that is actually quite a loving attitude". That was nice of her to say.

Plus, to be brutally honest, not many girls will say, "Ooo, I want my African-American child raised by that heavy-set Irish couple!"

And don't think I'm being misogynistic by saying "girls". Most of the birthmothers are girls — one of Marta's birthmothers turned fourteen during her pregnancy.

We liked the interview, we liked Marta; and agreed to their services. Within days we received their contract and signed and returned it with the first installment of our fees.

The sticker shock made me pause. The cost is almost prohibitive, considering the little spent on the fertilization treatments – we had mandatory insurance coverage, remember.

Esther was worried about pouring so much money into this and I rationalize it by saying, "With a child we'll have to get used to money flowing out of our bank account like a sieve!" But we couldn't make light of it. It was a lot of money we didn't have.

The Adoption Network has its own financing through GE Money Bank and we applied for a line of credit. Our second counselor, Cary (we got different counselors the deeper we went in the process – Cary ended up being the one we contacted the most), was surprised we got approved right away in this time of financial stress. "Let's face it," I had to brag, "With what I do for a living, I expected no problems." No problems getting the loan, but paying for it...

No interest for six month, then eleven percent after that. Eleven! That's almost three times what my car is. I have credit cards with less interest! So after six months, guess what's getting transferred to the old Citibank!

We are adopting just in time. Until 2010, just less than $11,000.00 of all money spent on adoption (fees, costs, postage, classes, home study, etc.) can be used as a tax credit from income on your Federal return. A credit, mind you, not a deduction, taken off the first page from the gross! And you can spread the credit through the years — four thousand this year, four thousand the next, etc.; although I expect we'll be able to use the entire credit. Add to this the extra deduction for the child and the child tax credit...

Well, like I said, I wasn't worried about getting approved for a loan...

Oh, and the credit was extended past 2010, just so you know.

⁓

*W*e received the contract and a huge packet of information on the evening of January 19, 2012.

The next day was inauguration day. Esther and I took the day off to watch the patriotic festivities and especially the parade. The son of two of my best friends from law school and undergrad rode in the parade as part of Culver Academy.

We reviewed and signed all the necessary paperwork while the festivities continued. We watched the President being sworn in and waited for the parade to start. It took some time. So we went to my office to fax the paperwork to California and then to 9th Street for a celebratory dinner. It was done. We are adopting.

We recorded the parade on Tivo. Jay would be in the last row of riders, second from left. When we heard Culver Academy was coming I grabbed the remote with my thumb on the pause/slow button. Row after row of young men on their gallant steeds passed the screen. In the back we saw the final row before the next equestrians.

Fortunately the camera was angled on the left side. We'll get a spot-on view of him! Here they come! There's his leg ... and ...

They cut to the next participants. A girl's equestrian school. WHAT!? "Oo, we only have one row of Culverites left, let's cut away to the pretty girls," the director said. Damn!! Well, we knew Jay was there – we saw his leg! His proud parents Jim and Cyndi knew he was there, too. They were in Washington to watch their son – well, a few miles away amidst the throng, but they were there...

Talk about an once-in-a-lifetime opportunity and honor. He has something to tell his children about; and hopefully soon, we will have our own child to tell.

⌒

The first thing we had to do was an FBI background check. FBI? We're adopting a baby not running an Al Qaida cell. If we had a baby the natural way we could have a meth lab in the garage and no one would bat an eye, but adopting... no!

We have to do this quickly – it takes a long time and we don't want the background check to stall any other process. What if we were picked next week?

Our prints were taken at the police department. The officer who helped us was very nice. He knew we weren't the usual scumbags who crossed his path. He still manhandled our fingers onto the inky pad. He twisted all my fingers at the knuckle. Ouch! I tried relaxing my hand to make his job easier, but reflexively I fought him. He didn't seem to mind. At least WE were sober and/or conscious.

The prints were mailed to Adoption Law Network and from there to the FBI, "Now ees finally time for truth, da?" I told Esther.

"I don't think you have anything to worry about," she said.

"Says you, capitalist peeg," Coincidentally my cousin Sam, who was himself adopted, was caught selling blue jeans when he visited the Soviet Union in 1987. They questioned him and let him go. He managed to sneak out some coins for me and a flag for him (with the blue bar — flown only within the Evil Empire).

Sam IMed me when we were playing World of Warcraft. "My mother said you are adopting."

"Yes."

"Are you crazy? I was adopted you know."

"Yes, but we won't adopt someone like YOU..."

Come to think of it, I haven't heard from Sam since. I hope I didn't hurt his feelings, I was kidding. I love ya, bro! Er, cuz!

⌐

*N*ext were the list of instructions, follow-up emails and a telephone call from Cary. We had to prepare three birthmother letters for their three websites, three paragraphs describing us, our home and our family; and answer a long questionnaire.

The three birthmother letters were all variations on a theme. We looked at letters from their website and adoption books and cobbled it together:

"Our names are Mike & Esther and we thank you for reading our letter! We hope you get to know us through this letter, our photos and other information on this page. Our sincerest hope is that you come to know and feel the love and affection we have for each other and the love and affection we want to share with a precious child as a result of your loving gift of adoption.

We are so grateful that you seek a loving family to raise and nurture your child. We also appreciate how difficult this time in your life must be as you consider adoption and we are praying that you will be given grace, guidance and peace as you make your decision.

Let me tell you about my Esther. All of my friends, family and co-workers adored Esther from the moment I introduced her to them. They were as taken by her gentleness, kindness and sweet disposition as I was. In 2000, she started working part-time as a librarian and is now in a management-level position there. She is taking classes part-time over the internet for her second Masters degree. When we started at our new church some years ago she was invited to sing with the choir in our third week there. And no wonder: she has a voice like an angel – having majored in singing at the seminary she attended. I am looking forward to sharing her kind and loving heart with you and your gift of adoption. Family and friends are unanimous in saying what a wonderful mother she will be. I can't wait until the child is old enough to appreciate Esther's cooking, especially her chowders and stews! Religion is very important to Esther – it came down to her from her parents (her brother was the minister at our wedding) – and I know she will also instill the love of God's grace in a precious baby. She is so brave and strong; I am very proud of her.

I first met Mike (or Michael, as his relatives have called him since childhood) in 1996. I decided he would make a good friend when he made me laugh at an evening with mutual friends for games and socializing. We dated in 1999, immediately knew we were a match and married in 2000. Mike is a successful attorney and has taken me on tours of many courthouses including the appellate court and our state supreme court. Before that he was a radio announcer – he was the radio spokesman for a sandwich store chain (although it was only six stores at the time) with commercials airing in Chicago and elsewhere. He still narrates our Easter and Christmas programs at our church and has done radio commercials for the library at which I work. I love to watch him play with children. He has such a rapport with his nieces and nephews and the children of his cousins – whether it's discussing grandparents or great-grandparents who are no longer with us or imitating Yoda and Kermit the Frog. Mike has an amazing gift of puppetry; whether with actual puppets or making a "doggie" with his hand. On one occasion he was pretending our cats were "arguing" with each other and I actually stepped in to stop them! "Nebula, stop teasing." Mike still teases me about that! Mike is so kind and loving and loyal – his sisters, cousins and friends were all so happy with our decision to adopt because they know what a good father he will be and what a good provider he already is.

When we were married in 2000, our favorite saying was "today I will marry my best friend; the one I laugh with, live for, dream with, love." That is as true today as it was 9 years ago. And it will be true with any child we are privileged enough to adopt. He or she will be nurtured and raised in a house filled with love, laughter and music. We have both been very blessed to have each other, and we want to share that blessing with a little one. Your wonderful gift to us will be raised in a home where the word "love" is heard more often than any other. We are very sentimental: we celebrate "monthiversaries" of birthdays and other special events – any excuse to lavish love and affection on each other and our friends and family. We also have a strict "hug on demand" rule in the house: hugs must be given at any time and for any reason upon request – no exceptions!

We both have a love of learning and an appreciation of history. We also love to travel; mostly to museums or other historic sites. We also stop at every antique shop and flea market on the way!

We promise you that your child will be raised with love and affection in a house filled with laughter and joy. He or she will be nurtured and cared for by us and our extended family and friends. We thank you so much for your consideration."

Wow, who farted? The questionnaire was equally gushy. I managed to keep my answers. Esther's answers were probably stored on her long-since-fried laptop.

Define "family life". "It means associating and having fellowship with a core group of people (not necessarily related to you) who share our values and beliefs, for whom and with whom we laugh, care and love."

Describe our childhood: "Mike was raised in a very small town by a stay-at-home mom and a father in the Air Force. He was raised with two sisters. He loved school and was president of his senior class. Being from such a small town and school instilled in him values such as a strong loyalty to home, church and to friends he still keeps in contact with 26 years later!"

We were asked to describe our home: "We live in a tri-level home with three bedrooms, two baths and a large basement. Throughout the year you can hear music and laughter in the house. On cool nights, we like to sit on the back porch with the chiminea blazing as we snuggle on the swing. We have a huge fenced-in backyard with another lot beside it – plenty of room for soccer, Frisbee and games of catch."

What do we do on a 3-day weekend: "Occasionally we like to spend over-night at the nearby city (about 90 miles away) for a night of dining, shopping and movies. We usually spend the extra time enjoying each other's company while working around the house."

Do we have pets? "Nebula, the kind and motherly alpha cat of the pack who has adopted Mike as her favorite kitten. Warlock, who loves to have his belly rubbed. Mao, a very vocal cat who is always thinks she's hungry even when she's not. And shy Fizzy, a gray Main Coon who got compliments on his beauty by a cat breeder we met at a wedding."

What is your favorite food? "Mike - his wife's lasagna or a pizza with nearly everything on it! Esther - Clam Chowder, Salmon, most seafood."

What will you teach your children? "To be a caring, active and productive member of society; that it is the individual's responsibility to care for the lesser members of society as per Christ's teachings and to develop the skills to do what they want in life and to attain their goals."

Do you play any musical instruments? "Esther can play the piano, French horn and trumpet and singing was her undergraduate major in college. Mike can play the guitar, piano and trumpet and is learning the violin ("fiddle," he insists). He also practices on a didgeridoo, much to the annoyance of the cats!"

Describe our neighborhood: "We live in a tri-level home in the historic district of our town. It is the newest house on the block and it was built in 1963. We are within walking distance of the library, the courthouse and down-town shops. We live in a large town in a rural area."

Share something about your spouse that only you know: "If I told you that, I would not be the only person who knew it!" *(I decided to keep this answer if only to forewarn the birthmother what a prat her child was getting for a dad...)*

Describe your last romantic thing you did? "(Answered by the Adoptive Dad) I took her to the nearby city's symphony orchestra to see and hear the Lord of the Rings Symphony. I did not tell her where we were going or what we were seeing. Fortunately neither the marquis nor the cover of the playbill revealed what was being performed that night. It was a complete surprise to her until the first note was played. Then we went to a wonderful outdoor restaurant by a lake (it was nearly midnight) for a romantic and perfect cap to a perfect evening!"

What will you tell your child about their birthmother? "As much as we know! We will keep all letters and photographs in a scrapbook (or DVD or who knows what kind of technology by then!) to share with our child."

What does Daddy do on a special day? "If weather permits, we will go outside and play until it is time to come in and enjoy his favorite thing to eat – his wife's lasagna!"

Do you plan on sharing with your child what their birth parents were like? "Yes, it is the child's right to know."

Describe the kind of education you hope to provide for your child? "In our area, the public schools provide a better and more rounded education than the private ones. Of course, education goes on 24 hours per day. Our adopted child will always be learning, just as the adopting parents are always learning."

Why did you decide to adopt? "We have been married for eight years and have tried to have a child through insemination and other infertility treatments. We feel that we have much love to give to a little one and could give a child a full and happy life. Also, it will be wonderful to have grandchildren to spoil and it will complete our family. I pour so much love on my wife, and she pours so much love into my heart – imagine how much love both of us together can give a child."

What faith will you raise your child? "Christian, non-denominational (as the Adoptive Mom was raised)."

Describe how you will help your child accomplish their dreams? "We will encourage our child to discover and use their talents at their pace and direction. Also (to be perfectly frank), our income even with a child is twice the mean income for our state for a family of three. The costs of providing the child with the means to discover his or her talents – whether musical, athletic, artistic, etc. – will not be a discouraging factor."

What kind of a relationship will you have with the birthmother through her pregnancy? "To gain her trust and friendship and to encourage her brave decision. We hope she will realize she will be giving her child a loving home and a wonderful and hope-filled future."

How did you meet? "A mutual friend introduced us at a weekend party of games and fellowship. This same group of friends meet up nearly every weekend fourteen years later." (*I was afraid mentioning we met playing Advanced Dungeons & Dragons would repel a Christian birthmother. "Oh, you're Satanists?"*)

Describe your relationship with your parents? "My father was the breadwinner and was gone from before we woke in the morning until dinner time in the evening. My mother was the disciplinarian in the household. My mother was fiercely protective of our safety and our mental well being, whereas my father was a gentle and quiet man with a strong sense of humor. As I matured into adulthood I became protective of my mother as she grew older and feebler. Since she first contracted cancer and passed away in 2001 she has always been in my thoughts. Her love for me was absolute and unconditional and she was my biggest supporter in anything I did. Except for my lovely wife, Esther, I would give all I have for just a few more minutes sitting by her chair hearing her hum one of her songs. My father and I have become close friends since I have become an adult. I'm proud to have him as my father; were he not my father I'm still proud to have him as a friend; were he not my friend I'd still be proud he was a member of the community. In 2007 he was selected as his town's Citizen of the Year. My thought was not only should he be honored, but also the town should be honored for recognizing what a wonderful man he is. He is my hero."

What attracted you to each other? "She has the cutest nose and a cute round little face which I love to smooch. She was always very kind and sweet to me even when we were friends before it turned more romantic. She's also very intelligent. If nothing else, she has a cute giggle."

Please describe your personalities: "Adoptive Mom? Very kind and gentle. Has a voracious need to learn new things and to immerse herself into any subject she is interested in. Optimistic, but with a logical street sense that brings a cautionary thoughtfulness -- so she is rarely impulsive. Very patient, but doesn't put up with intentionally bad behavior. She enjoys planning and knowing what will happen in the future – whether it's what is for dinner or what will we be doing this weekend. It's very hard to surprise her (but when she is surprised no one is more pleased that her)." *(I let Esther describe me. I don't know what she said. I hope it was nice...)*

Describe your hobbies: "Collecting (and playing with) antique toys, collecting (and reading) antique books and comic books. Any and all things relating to the Beatles. He also plays guitar. He loves reading fiction and biographies; he writes short fiction and novels (one item published so far) and enjoys buying and selling on ebay. Over the last year he has enjoyed playing World of Warcraft with his cousin and his fellow employees! With the Adoptive Mom, he enjoys antique shops and flea markets."

Adoptive Mom: When are holding your baby what are your thoughts on the birthmother? "How lucky she was to have had such a lovely child. How lucky we are to have been selected to adopt the child by this brave and wonderful young woman. It was a momentous and valiant decision to put the needs of her child ahead of anything else."

How will a child enrich your life? "There's a saying that your spouse is the only member of your family that you are allowed to choose. But an adopted child is too. And through the birthmom, the baby in a way chooses you! We pour so much love into each other's hearts more and more every day, can you imagine how much love each of us can pour into a precious child? A child will allow us to continue to love each other, but to double our love onto a young life. At marriage, two become one. With this adoption, another will be added. Our house filled with love and laughter will be enhanced a thousand times with the love and laughter of a growing child. He or she will be our best friend, our student, our teacher, our ward, our caretaker. Once I said to my wife, 'you are the greatest love of my life; a baby will be the greatest love of our lives.'"

Describe your career and why you chose that path: "I have wanted to be an attorney since I was a young teenager. The law continues to bring intellectual challenges every day, as well as the privilege to help those who might not have a voice or be able to help themselves in the morass the law often times finds itself. I wanted to be a guide to those who might become frustrated at all the red tape. I come from an area of the country where attorneys are still respected leaders in their community and I have always consider being an asset to my community a requirement to being a citizen of a community. And let's face it, the money isn't bad!!" *(I couldn't resist mentioning filthy lucre – I do not make as much as I hinted at here, but I wanted the birthmother to know her baby would not want for anything. Unless she wanted a Porsche…)*

What makes a birthmother special? "As the Adopting Mom said before, the birthmom is a selfless and brave young woman who thinks of the needs and wants of her precious gift by allowing him or her to be adopted by a loving and caring family. Birthmoms should be lauded for the happiness she has brought to the child and to the adopting family. She should never be forgotten!" *(I tried to be as fawning as I could, although I do not really like that question. What if the birthmother was a skanky crack-whore – as opposed to a glamorous crack-whore - whose child was taken away by the state?).*

The Three Descriptive Paragraphs:

About us

Mike and Esther met in 1996 and were married in 2000. Esther is the Assistant Head Librarian in our town (it employs 15 librarians) and enjoys reading and crafts – making jewelry especially. She sings in the church choir every week and solos during special programs. She enjoys current affairs and keeps up on the national and international news and events. Music is very evident in her background and enjoys singing along with her favorite Contemporary Christian songs. Mike is a successful attorney and also enjoys reading and listening to music – especially the Beatles. He writes short fiction and novels of many genres – mystery, speculative and thriller especially – and has recently wrote some historical and non-fiction pieces. He plays guitar, piano and trumpet and is learning the violin. He likes to collect antique toys, books and comics and buying and selling the ones he doesn't want to keep for himself on ebay!

As seen in the photos, we still share as much or more affection and love for each other as on the day we wed. The phrase they hear the most from new friends and even a couple they met in Ireland is that they are a "cute couple". They enjoy traveling and going to museums and historic sites. They also stop at every antique store and flea market they pass!

Together we love to laugh and share stories and tell each other about our day. We are both very lucky – not everyone gets to marry their best friend! We give each other so much love and are looking forward to also giving that love to a precious child. Mike once said, "Marrying you was the happiest day of my life."

"What about the day we have a baby?" Esther asked.

"That will be the happiest day in our lives."

Home

Our home sits on three lots with a huge fenced-in back yard with plenty of room for a young child to run and play. A huge playground swing set and slide will look very nice between the shady magnolia and the walnut tree. We have an extra lot beyond for games of soccer, Frisbee and catch.

We live in a tri-level home in the historical district of our town. We have the newest house in our quiet neighborhood – built in 1963! We live within 5 blocks of the library (where Esther works), the courthouse and the high school (the only one in the town), but several miles away from the commercial/service areas of town (fast food, theaters, department stores, etc.).

Family

If we are privileged enough to be selected by a birth mother, this will be our first child. But this doesn't mean the baby will be without a large family. Some generalizations are true: Mike's Irish heritage means that he has incredibly strong ties to his extended family (his father helped to get a teaching position in his town for his nephew's daughter. How many other people would even know the name of their brother's grandchild let alone know them well enough to recommend them for a job?). Two or three times per year the families get together for reunions and dinners. The baby will have 17 cousins, five under the age of nine. He or she will also have 10 second (and third) cousins all under the age of seven. Mike's sister is already planning the baby shower on "arrival day". Esther's father lives nearby and we are frequent visitors for dinner (both of our mothers have passed away), but the rest of her brothers and sisters live several hundreds of miles away, but contact is kept with them through phone calls and floods of emails!

A little thick, isn't it? Well, it seems to be what they were looking for.

The main thing I disliked was the deification of the birth mother – considering her a saint; a mix of Mother Mary, Joan of Arc and Gaia. Yes a birthmother is courageous and noble and making the ultimate sacrifice, but I wanted to be honest.

I really wanted to say, "I know you are scared shitless. You don't know what to do; you don't know where to go. I wish I could give you want you want, but you probably don't know what you want. I am so sorry for whatever brought you here and I wish I could go back in time and help you prevent it. But I can promise we will take care of your baby. He or she will grow up to be as kind and gentle and tough and strong as Esther. And I will protect him or her with the ferocity of an injured bear!

"Neither of us can begin to know the feelings you are feeling right now. All I can say is that your baby will be loved and cherished until the day we die and if you choose us I guarantee you will always be in our and your baby's minds and hearts.

"Good luck."

I wonder how many responses we would get if I had said that?

⟋⟍

*W*e also needed 35 photographs.

Odd number, 35. One of our home, one of our pets, 6 "action shots" of each of us and 6 "action shots" of us together and the rest various close ups. No problem! Pictures of us at the Blarney Stone (we went on a consolation vacation to Ireland in 2005 – it was my third visit to the Emerald Isle, Esther's second – she and I first went together in mid-September 2001. Yes, THAT mid-September 2001. In the midst of all that happened that mid-September we were went to Ireland. Fun flight.), us at the ocean, at Lincoln's Tomb, at renaissance fairs, woo hoo!

Then we read the instructions: photographs must be within the past year. Uh-oh.

With Esther's first year working full time, we didn't go anywhere in the previous year!

The disk with the photos had to be sent to them within 30 days; 8 of which had already passed. So we spent the weekend of January 30th taking lots of photos.

January in southern Illinois is not bad. It gets cold – hovering in the 30s, rarely getting below freezing during the day. If you wear a jacket or a thick shirt, you should be okay.

So of course on January 26th we got eight inches of snow.

Our house was blanketed in white. We took pictures throwing snowballs at each other and shoveling the white stuff. We took photos at work and eating at our Saturday restaurant (a tradition, remember?) and at church. Esther bought a tripod that morning and we took photos of us by the fireplace, me on the guitar and serenading Nebula the cat with my violin; Esther with her jewelry kit. We dug out the Simpson's Game of Life, set it up and photographed our playing it.

We went to the garage and photographed ourselves in shorts on the lawnmower where you couldn't tell there was snow (it was seventeen degrees — we wanted this badly!).

Snow doesn't last long here, so within a week it had melted and we could take some real outdoor shots. We went to the local museum with a friend who took pictures of us in front of the various works of art and outside amongst the statuary. One photo I liked was in the children's section – a large glass window with markers and erasers for the potential Van Goghs to show their temporary work. The photo is of my writing "I (heart) Esther" in thick black marker. I have a nice smile on my face. Esther loved it, too.

No photos with hats, masks or sunglasses were allowed, said the rules. Tough noogies. We had a few photos from the previous summer during my family reunion; we were wearing sunglasses. We submitted them anyway, hoping they wouldn't get on us. "Hey, can't you read?!"

We worried. Action photos? I get winded getting out of bed. What kind of action shots are they talking about? A photo of me jogging? When I run I look like a lava lamp. A photo of me hunting? Even Ted Nugent would agree I should be banned from owning a gun. "Give me that rifle before you kill someone! Go home!" I don't even own a basketball or a baseball – what was I supposed to do?

We looked through the websites of the awaiting families and stopped worrying. Some "action" photos included playing board games and making dinner. One person was parasailing in the far distance! You couldn't tell who it was! Those cheating bastards!

I found a cool photo of a guy in a shark cage fending off a great white, but Esther said no. Neither did she allow my photo-shopped picture of me shaking hands with Franklin Roosevelt, "LBJ did it! And he did it without the use of a computer!" I argued. Well, probably for the best, I guess. They'd probably suspect that one.

We decided to ask about one photo in particular.

During the summer of 2004 our friends Clyde and Virginia celebrated their twentieth wedding anniversary. I had known them for eight years and Esther had known them for eleven. We shared an interest in old comic books, role playing games, Dr. Who, Star Trek and all things nerdy. I ooh and aah over his collection of Captain Action figures; he over my Mego collection. Both of us collect DVDs of Saturday morning cartoons and hope to re-enact a morning from the late 1960s – watching our cartoons and munching on Quisp. They still make Quisp you know. I found some in Indiana.

They decided to renew their vows. It would be a fantasy/medieval theme. They asked a few Renaissance Fairs if they could have the ceremony there, but that would be too expensive and/or they couldn't accommodate a party that small.

They held the wedding at Boo Rothman Park south of Carbondale, Illinois. Boo Rothman was a young man in his twenties who was killed in a car crash some years before. His father bought the land where Boo was killed and built a park. Boo was also into Dungeons & Dragons, Lord of the Rings and such nerdliness; and his father built the park with that theme. He built and placed statues based on Boo's painted miniature figures. A huge stone dragon sat near the entrance. He built an adult-sized play castle – complete with a rope bridge and a secret tunnel in which lurked an orc; lots of places for young and old to climb and enjoy. It was perfect.

Clyde asked me to be best man, Esther the matron of honor. Their teenage daughter Virginia was maid-of-honor. Our mutual friend Doug, a minister, would preside.

Doug and I were class mates in law school in 1989. We had lots of classes together and became good friends. When I moved to Mount Vernon in January of 1996 (why do big things always seem to happen in January...) he called me. He lived in a small town nearby and asked if I wanted to join him in an evening of gaming.

Sure! I had been in town about four months and it would be nice to make some friends. I followed him to a house in an even smaller town near Mount Vernon and was introduced to "The Gamers".

Role playing gamers – Dungeons and Dragons, Traveller, Chill, DC Superheroes, Call of Cthulhu, Star Wars, you name it. The house belonged to Tom and Lisa and their kids (who also gamed as they got older) Kyle and Kristen; Allen, Don, Steve (and eventually his wife Linda), Esther...

Cue violin music, wistful glances...

...and her husband Joe.

Wonk.

It was neither that simple nor that romantic. No thunderbolt. She was a friend of Doug's. A married friend of Doug's. Oh she was as cute as a button, but there was no romantic (or other) feelings for her other than she was a friend of a friend.

Her being part of the crowd, I don't remember meeting Esther specifically. The first time I remember her speaking directly to me was the next week. I missed the turn to Tommy and Lisa's house, turned the car around and came in from the east, rather than the west. We each drove onto Tommy and Lisa's driveway at the same time.

"Do you live down that way," Esther said.

"No, I missed the turn," I said.

"Oh, I have family living down that road and thought you might live that way, too," she said.

Thus was the first conversation with the love of my life.

What Esther did not know was Joe was falling for another woman on an online role-playing game (called a "MUSH" - Multi-User Shared Hallucination a pun on MUD – multi-user dungeon). He left Esther by that summer and eventually married the other woman. They are still married as far as we know and happy. Good for him.

Although she eventually forgave him, it tore Esther apart. It took her two years to muster the resolve to divorce him. She asked Doug to help with the paperwork. She filed and was granted a divorce in October 2009.

A week or so after the divorce, I said something that made her laugh. She shared half of her sandwich with me. The next week she made potato soup for the Gamers. By November 8th, she asked me out on a date.

I was in love with her by Thanksgiving and proposed New Year's Day.

Cue violin music, wistful glances…

Four years later, at Clyde and Virginia's vow renewal, Esther wore her wedding dress – toned down a bit and with appropriate medieval trappings. I rented my costume of green wool from Johnny Brock's Dungeon in St. Louis. Doug dressed as a monk. Virginia made her, Britanny's and Clyde's costumes. We looked like we stepped off the set of "Camelot".

Winter in southern Illinois is mild.

Summer is hellish.

That's not quite true – calling summer in southern Illinois hellish would be an insult to Satan's warm and cozy domain. Southern Illinois hits 90 usually in mid-June and stays there until mid-September, with about a week in the hundreds for good measure. The humidity is right up there too.

But the day of the wedding was in the 70s with low humidity. That is about as rare as … well … eight inches of snow in January. So there we were in our wool tunics, hats and pants, leather boots, crinoline and such enjoying a summer day one only sees in MGM musicals. Usually, our summer days are more like "African Queen" or "Bad Day at Black Rock".

The wedding was lovely and the guests enjoyed themselves. A cameraman from the local newspaper was there and on Monday we were in living color on the front page of the regional section.

We took lots of photos, too. One showed Esther and I arm in arm standing at the front entrance of the wooden castle. Our smiles lit up the picture.

And that was the photo we wanted to submit for our adoption portfolio.

By January of 2009 the photo was over a year old. Against the rules.

Esther emailed the photo on February 4th with this note: "As far as the last picture--it is about four years old. It is one of our favorite pictures of us. We were attendants at our best friends' renewal of their wedding vows for their 20th anniversary. It was a Renaissance themed wedding--and we attend Ren Faires most years, but don't get to dress up. So this really shows who we are-- plus I am wearing my wedding dress in this picture. I know that you may not use it, but I did want to make my case for sending it."

That very day we got this response from our new counselor, Stacy: "Hi Esther, I appreciate your email. You can relax and know that we will build a fabulous webpage that reflects who you are and will benefit you."

Not exactly a yes, not exactly a no. This was neither an agency nor a facilitator, I decided, it was a law firm.

But they used the photo.

We spent Sunday night filling in the questionnaire and completing the letters and descriptive info, put it all on a disk and mailed it out Tuesday the third of February. Some of the captions for the pics were: Mike serenades Nebula (one of our cats – I was playing the violin with her in the foreground), attending friend's period wedding, Mike's office, at Lincoln's Tomb, G'day Nebula – d'ye like my didgeridoo? (don't ask), winter snuggles, Esther making jewelry, hugs on demand, Mike's 3 favorite gals (take it easy, it was Esther and two of the cats), on vacation, Esther at work, Warlock in bed (another cat, what's the matter with you? Get out of the gutter for god's sake…).

By late February our three pages were ready, up and running! At the time their addresses were www.adoptionnetwork.com, www.courageouschoice. com, and www.adoptionspacebook.com. The websites randomizes the couples, so the same ones aren't always first. We liked that.

You can search by region, ethnicity or religious preference. If I wanted my child to be adopted by an Hispanic Muslim couple from Idaho, I could find them. They are probably living in a condo with bigfoot and Elvis, but … you never know.

The average wait time is four months for a "match". Our counselors (we have had five now – Marta, Cary, Stacy, Laura and Laura) said we could be picked as early as May!

So we wait to be picked. What do we do in the meantime? Cue spooky music and deep modulated voice: "You thought you had lots of redundant forms and fees up until now? Welcome to Illinois..."

Three

PICKED!

"Joking on the square" means you are just kidding, but also serious. When you joke on the square, what you say is couched in humor but you mean what is said.

So when I talk about bureaucratic red tape, I am joking on the square.

The government side of adopting was no different than that required by the firm/agency/facilitator – fees, forms, fees, classes, fees, inspections and fees.

The Adoption Network Law Center gave us a list of agencies we could use for the Illinois side of things. We picked Lutheran Child and Family Services. Esther worked with a lot of these services during her counseling days and liked LCFS. Our counselor/agent was named Helen.

Esther was very happy with that – she knew Helen and they had a lot of mutual friends and former co-workers. Helen remembered Esther too – this saved the trouble of the getting-to-know-one-another phase. It would not be a perfect stranger deciding what kind of parents we would make.

The Illinois Department of Children & Family Services required another set of fingerprints.

"Couldn't you use the set we had already sent to the FBI?"

"No, this has to be new fingerprints."

"In case they've changed?"

"No, we have to use a specific company to take and process your prints."

"Ah, I see." I'm sure if I check the list of stockholders of this "specific company" I'll find names similar to the upper echelon of Illinois lawmakers who enacted the law. There's no money to be made if they use the same prints, you see.

So during my lunch break it was off to the local DCFS office to take my fingerprints electronically. I watched the clock tick away my lunch hour. With twenty minutes to spare I was ushered into a room where a very friendly lady took each of my fingers and pressed them onto a pad and then onto a computer screen. No rolling black ink onto a tray, no industrial carcinogenic goo to clean my fingers as was done at the police station some months before. She was gentler about rolling my fingers across the pad than the police officer, but that was understandable. He usually had uncooperative fingerprintees and he was rough out of habit.

I made it back in time for my next appointment. Esther had her fingerprints taken later that day.

We each had to provide a self-study. This meant several essay questions about our lives and interests.

We had to describe our schooling:

"I enjoyed high school very much and made mostly "A"s with a few "B"s. I was president of senior class and a member of the band and drama club, was a newspaper staff artist and yearbook writer. I was one of two Illinois Scholars from our school. I won the Best Actor Award in 1982. Also in 1982 I was won the DAR Good Citizenship Award (Note: I was told at the time that I was one of the first boys to win the once-girl-only award, but I have not in all these years been able to prove that).

"During my high school years I was also awarded the Kappa Kappa Psi Citation for Musical Excellence and the Southern Illinois Good Student Award. Being a small school we formed deep friendships with each other and I still keep in touch with most of my high school classmates.

"I also enjoyed college – being able to study the subjects that interested me was one of its main highlights. I drew comic strips and editorial cartoons for the university newspaper, helped form a student advertising/

media production club and was active in the local public radio station. I also helped proctor examinations for students with learning disabilities. My favorite activity was drawing a daily comic strip for the university newspaper. I am still proud of the series and keep the original inks in a safe place.

"I did not enjoy law school as much as high school or college because of its very strict policies of class attendance and participation. I expected more freedom in the way one learns.

"But it was obviously necessary to become an attorney. Personally I wished they would have treated us as the adults we were. I felt like I was given more latitude in high school. This was because the Law School was young and still had to "prove" it's worth to the state bar, I suppose. I continued to proctor exams and work in public radio as I did in undergrad, but was also voted Third Year President and was instrumental in getting Secretary of State Roland Burris as our commencement speaker. I received the class high grade in Education Law and Third-Year Writing. As little as I enjoyed the school, I loved the comradery with my classmates. I have kept in touch with most of my classmates and was in charge of our recent 15-year reunion."

... our families:

"Dad is a very quiet and gentle man. He worked most of the day and when he got home he mostly listened to baseball and hockey games on the radio. My favorite times with him were in the morning before he left when we would listen to the morning news and watch "The Lone Ranger" together. He would rarely discipline any of us and (being of that generation) did not show physical signs of love to us – although he raised us to know that his love and affection for us was limitless. I and my sisters got closer to him as we grew older. My father is one of my closest friends and we telephone each other weekly. I still ask for his advice and counsel on most issues – including this adoption.

"Mom was the disciplinarian of the household. She wanted to keep a clean and quiet household and would discipline us verbally and physically when we disobeyed (modern note: no more than a spanking, don't get me wrong...). As we grew old enough to move out of the house she grew kinder and as an adult I loved visiting with her, going out to eat, helping her with her genealogy research. Not a day goes by that I do not miss her."

...our childhood/young adulthood and adulthood:

"I have realized while preparing this self-study that my interests in Childhood/Young Adult/Adulthood have basically remained unchanged. I always have been an avid reader and was writing science/mystery/thriller fiction since I was a child. I created comic books of the characters I read about.

"I loved to draw and did so even into my college career. My favorite memories of college were writing and drawing the daily comic strip for the university newspaper.

"Music was another passion during my life. When my brother went into the Air Force he gave me his albums – mostly Beatles and Rolling Stones. This love of music lead to my career in radio which began in college and continued for ten years after which I left the field to begin my legal career – I was still in the radio business until four months before my law school graduation.

"I began playing the trumpet in the grade school band in 1975. Since then I have learned to play the piano and guitar and am currently learning the violin.

"In recent years I still play and listen to music and read and write fiction. I also love to travel (I have been to Europe four times), usually to historic sites and museums.

"The toys and comics I played with and read as a child are now collections encased in glass and plastic. I still love to collect comics and antique toys and am also selling books, comics, toys, coins and stamps on ebay."

... and religion (odd thing to ask in a governmental form, but still ...):

"My family was raised Presbyterian and has been since at least the nineteenth century when my great-grandfather left northern Ireland for America. My grandfather was a deacon/elder at the church we attended for over sixty years (he was 94 when he died in 1970). He, my father (his son) and all my aunts, uncles and most of my cousins were baptized in the same Reformed Presbyterian Church, Evangelical Synod which still stands today.

"Although as a youth I enjoyed going to the church and being with my friends, it was not a youth-oriented church – quite the opposite in fact. As a teenager, I became frustrated by its lack of programs for young people and the elder's discouragement of teen meetings and outings to movies, amusement parks, etc. They also had strict rules against young people participating in church affairs.

"During college and onward organized religion held no interest to me. Although I even then considered myself religious and spiritual, I considered the compartmentalization of modern religion as more part of its problem.

"When I met my wife Esther she showed me how important religion was in her life. I am the type of person who believes that if it is important to her, it is therefore important to me. So I started attending church with her. I was impressed that many of the draconian rules of dress and behavior and much of the dogmatic systems did not exist in her church. It was not without its problems: I became frustrated at the egotistic and authoritarian beliefs that so dominated the church and so-called Christian leaders in the past decade. In one breath they would say how we must love everyone and in the next spout such vitriolic and phobic hatred of others simply because their beliefs did not match "ours". We were told that some people are ungodly because of who they voted for. I was in that category. From the pulpit, the associate minister said I was just "going through the motions" and did not really have Christ in my heart. I have yet to return to that church. Fortunately, Esther decided to leave that church the next Wednesday when that same minister, again from the pulpit, told the parishioners who to vote for.

"However, over two years ago we have found and continue to attend a wonderful church that truly practices and follows Christ's teachings. If my church had been this way in 1982, I might not ever have left!"

Just like the bios prepared for our adoption web page, I saw it as a sales presentation. You had to tell the truth obviously, but I think they expect a self-study to be read through rose-colored glasses and to include a bit of bragging.

Otherwise, I'd be no different than the average applicant. "What is your favorite thing to do?" Really? I mean really? I sit in my recliner and try not to nod off until it is time to go to bed.

"What is your worst attribute?" Really? Motivation – you don't know how comfy this couch is on a Friday night after a long week.

"Describe your relationship with your parents." Do you mean the kind elderly people they became when I was an adult or the Klingons who raised me?

"What is your least favorite thing to do?" Other than write masturbatory biographies about me and my family? Ironing. God I hate ironing. I don't mind laundry, but rubbing my clothes with scalding hot metal just so they look like they haven't been slept in… Bleck.

Mowing, vacuuming, mopping – these are good things because they have positive results. You have a nice lawn, a neat house. Sometimes people even comment on it.

No one compliments you on ironing, though. But they snicker if you do NOT iron. "Jeez, did you fall asleep under yer car last night?"

You might get a "nice shirt", or a "that looks very good on you"; but never, never has anyone walked up and said, "my but you have nicely ironed apparel! What sharp creases!"

⌣

We were required to take a child-rearing class. So it was up at 5:30 am on Saturday, February 21st for our one-and-a-half hour drive to Belleville, Illinois to the LCFS office.

The city of Belleville has been my stomping grounds ever since I have been able to stomp. They had small used book stores, a Ben Franklin that still sold candy cigarettes well into the 1990s, and lots of corner taverns that served great food at lunch and dinner. One tavern sold brain sandwiches (calf's brains for you zombie-apocalypse weirdoes…). Another had a buffet at lunch set up on their pool table.

When we arrived it was raining. Soon there were eight of us huddled in the doorway waiting for them to open. Someone finally braved the cold rain and walked around the building and tried the back door. The counselors were waiting for us there. They opened the main entrance for the rest of us and started the all-day class.

The other couples came from Springfield, Decatur and deep in southern Illinois. Some stayed in motels and others had been driving since 3:00 am. Ick.

We learned about how and when a child develops, how they express themselves at all ages, the terrible twos, the even-more-terrible threes; that sort of thing.

Esther had some training in child development. One part of the class taught us how children play with (and without) each other. Our teacher described small children sitting with each other but otherwise playing with their own toys and not together as a group.

"Parallel play," Esther said.

"Yes, exactly," the teacher said. She stammered a bit. She did not expect anyone to use (or even know) that term. I've got one that can SEE!

There were lessons on how babies communicate with us and others, how toddlers, teens and adolescents communicate with parents and peers. Relatively, of course. Conversing with babies and teens has about the same effect as talking to your cat. Toddlers are a bit more receptive and responsive (even if the response is "NO!").

We learned about international adoption (one couple was adopting from South America) and adoption through the foster care system. Most of the couples taking the class – we totaled about twenty – were adopting internationally and were most interested in this session.

While interesting, we weren't that interested. We perked up when discussing the legalities involved afterward – the court documents, the court appearances and the reports from the child service organizations.

We each told our story. There was an elderly couple – retirees from southern Illinois – who were adopting a 16-year-old boy.

After lunch they brought in three couples who had completed their adoptions. They told their tales while the children squirmed on their laps or played with toys at their feet. One couple's child was from China, the others lived here in Illinois and adopted through the DCFS foster system.

We met an attorney who told us about the legal side of adopting. She didn't work for DCFS, but was one of several attorneys they use for processing the paperwork, court appearances and such. We mentioned we were going through Adoption Law Center Network.

"We need to talk," she said in a high-pitched voice while staring at the ceiling. Her hands were clasped behind her back as she bounced back and forth against the wall.

We were lectured about the evils of facilitators. Remember? If you are an agency, facilitators are Fagan-like baby brokers who will steal your money and leave you with diseased and crippled children if they leave you with one at all. That's why Illinois is making facilitators illegal, she said.

"Do we need to worry?" Esther wrote on a piece of paper during the harangue.

"No," I wrote back.

Later I said that if we went through the state agency she would be hired to do the paperwork instead of the Center hiring their attorney (they used an adoption attorney in Chicago).

"Never ask an encyclopedia salesman if you need a set of encyclopedias. And never EVER ask an encyclopedia salesman if you should buy them from another encyclopedia salesman," I said.

She tried scaring us into hiring her. It didn't work.

My favorite part of the class was an experiment in interracial relations: they gave us several different colored beads - white, black, brown, red, yellow - and a small Dixie cup. The speaker asked us several questions and we put the corresponding color in the cup. The color represented 60% or more: What is the predominant skin color of your neighborhood? Your church? The teachers at the school the child will attend? What color is your minister? Your dentist? Your doctor? (Ah, finally a brown bead for us - by this time we were getting the point) What is the color of the authors of the genre of books you read (I liked that one!)? Only one couple (the older couple adopting the 16-year-old) had more than three non-white colors in their cup when it was done. We only had one – my doctor. Try it!

⌒

The adoption has settled into a typical governmental "hurry up and wait" mode. Can't we just slip Blogojovich a couple of grand and skip all this? We waited for the home study to be finished and sent to the proper authorities. We waited for the FBI and state clearance based on our finger-print findings. We waited to be selected by a birthmother through our three webpages.

At least while we wait we can see how many people visit our websites - about 50 per month. Even if most of them are family, friends or other adopt-ing parents (either checking out the competition or copying our birth mother letters – just like we did), we guessed about 5-10 potential birthmothers are looking at us. That made us feel better.

We needed two hours of baby CPR classes. Baby CPR? How are they supposed to get their chubby baby arms around my torso? The lo-cal hospital chain offered baby CPR classes every month in the nearby town of Centralia. We signed up for the March class.

Esther and I were on separate work schedules so we each drove to the hospital on a dark Tuesday night. The room where the classes were held was locked. When Esther arrived, we walked to the lobby. The attendant, natu-rally, had no idea what we were talking about. "Baby CPR? We give Baby CPR classes? How do they get their chubby baby arms around your torso?" Neither did her supervisor. "Baby CPR classes? We give Baby CPR classes? How do their get their chubby baby arms around your torso?"

After a half-hour wait some phone calls were made. Seems the person holding the class decided to cancel without telling anyone. Well, without tell-ing anyone that could have called us and saved us a trip.

So we signed up for the April class. This time Esther and I managed our schedules to go together. Here's hoping someone is there, I said. We called that afternoon to make sure someone – anyone – would be there or at least knew what a Baby CPR class was. And to know how to get their chubby baby arms ...

And lo, the instructor was present; and Esther and I. No one else attended the class that evening. Just like the diabetes class from half a decade before, I was hoping to go through this anonymously. Let other people ask the ques-tions and volunteer. I just want to observe, throttle a mannequin and go home.

It was fun after all - blowing air into and beating the stuffing out of plastic dolls for three hours. We received our certificates a month later – and mailed copies to Helen and Cary.

As part of the class we earned one hour of credit at Rend Lake College. This is fantastic news: I had so very much wanted to take a class in the "00" decade and now I have done so. This means my academic career has spanned five decades — the 60s, 70s, 80s, 90s and 00s. I started my academic career in August of 1969 and finished in April of 2009 – oh there was a 17-year gap between 1992 and 2009, but it counts.

1969 versus 2009. Then and now.

Then: the Beatles released their album "Abbey Road" to great acclaim and great sales; Now: the Beatles: Rock Band game was released to great acclaim and great sales.

Then: the TV show *Star Trek* was cancelled due to poor ratings; Now: The movie "Star Trek" brought in 76 million dollars in its first weekend and was the #1 movie that spring week.

Then: the #1 movie that September was "Butch Cassidy and the Sundance Kid", featuring two legendary Hollywood stars; Now: Paul Newman died in September of the year before: one of the last legendary Hollywood stars.

Then: the #1 TV show was *Laugh In*: a seemingly shallow, silly show that hides a knowing satirical reflection of society; Now: the #1 TV show was *American Idol*: a shallow, silly show that is a sad reflection of society.

Then: the current US President would resign in disgrace after committing criminal acts; Now: the current governor of Illinois would resign in disgrace after committing criminal acts.

Then: a new president is inaugurated after the previous president, a Texan with some shady business partners involved us in a long and arduous war; Now: umm …

Then: the governor of California is a laughably bad actor who did make some good action flicks in his day; Now: umm …

My how times have changed.

*I*n late April we also had our home study. In Illinois, a home study is required to be licensed foster parents; and we have to be licensed foster parents to adopt.

So, a home study - a state agency has to "inspect" our home for cabinet locks, stairway blockers, sufficient living space and to make sure the Ajax is kept out of reach; that sort of thing.

I was late coming home from work during our Home Study so Helen and Esther spent the hour waiting for me reminiscing and chatting. Helen read a 17-page document spelling out the rights and responsibilities of birthmothers and foster parents. We had to initial every page when completed. We filled out a page listing the physical and mental ailments we would accept in a child (we had already done that for our adoption agency).

She toured the house with Esther while I made a diagram of our home. After two frustrating tries I copied the diagram from our appraisal when we bought the house in 2000. We measured the rooms and wrote in the dimensions.

Get this: in order to be approved a child's bedroom has to be no less than 40 square feet, 40!? And 35 square feet for every child thereafter. Old mobile homes from the 1970s may have had bedrooms that small — but I've been in bigger showers! We could house 4 children upstairs and 3 in the basement with those criteria...

Our final interview with Helen was on Saturday, May 23rd at her office. She talked to each of us privately. She asked me about my mother's death due to cancer (and Esther's mother), how Esther and I met, what attracted us to each other, etc.

She asked who would be the enforcer and who would be the softie — easy — I would be the softie. I can tell that just by the way I spoil the cats! Helen smiled.

I suspected why, and confirmed it on the drive home. Esther and I had given her identical answers. Esther's answer as to who would be the softie was the same as mine; word for word — including the "spoil the cats" line. We were pleased the meeting went well. Not that we were worried about being denied, but it was nice to know we wouldn't be rejected because of physical ("too old") or mental ("too crazy") or legal reasons ("Why do you buy batteries and antihistamine on a weekly basis?" "Well, that should be fairly obvious nowadays, I mean, wake up and smell the methamphetamine...").

Helen prepared the home study over the next few weeks. We asked for a copy, but we never received one.

On June 10, 2009 we became officially-licensed foster parents for the state of Illinois. We have our little cards good for the next four years. When we were told we had to be foster parents to adopt some months before I was worried. I imagined it like being on the rolls of the federal district court. At any time I might get drafted as a defense attorney in a federal criminal matter. He would win on appeal due to grossly incompetent representation – I would volunteer to be his star witness – but he would still be rotting in prison for the half-a-decade such an appeal would take.

"Does this mean a caseworker will knock on our door some morning with a 17-year-old hooligan that we'll have to watch until his court date?"

"No," said Helen. By now she was used to my catastrophic questions. "No one can force you to be a foster parent. This is just so you can adopt. But if you want to, you can."

"No," I said.

"Maybe," said Esther.

"Maybe," I said.

So we are now licensed foster parents. This means that our clearance was cleared and our home study was approved. All the red tape, forms, photos, classes and fees are done. Done and done.

We did not get our actual licenses until June 20th. We were approved for 2 children up to the age of three.

Now all we need is a child.

⁓

*I*n the meantime I enjoyed "History Channel International" as much as I could (now it is called "H2" – trying to be hip while airing shows on aliens, bigfoot, large machines and other bits of "history"). The next ten years television will consist of either muppet-like creatures or cartoon characters that teach kids belching is funny. This is a corollary to my initial observation of eating at nice restaurants while we can — the next ten years we won't be eating at any place whose décor doesn't include a brightly-colored slide.

⟍⟋

We wait to get picked by a birthmother. We were told we might be picked as early as May. May came and went. We were told the average wait time was four months. That deadline was fast approaching.

Should I worry? A silly question – of course I should worry. I worry about everything. I worry about having enough gas to get home when it's still a quarter full. I worry about Esther when she travels. I worry about the client sitting in the lobby waiting for his appointment. I worry about getting what I order when I am in a drive-through restaurant.

I worry about what will happen in court. I worry about getting to court on time – what if I get stuck behind some yokel at a red light and he uses this as an opportunity to start an Andy Griffith routine…

"Hey, that laht jes turned green! Ain't it a perty color? Let's stick around and see if it turns back… Aw!! It's yeller now! Oh! It's back to bein' red! Thet was quick. Who's that honkin' behind me? Now thet's jus' plain rude…"

And now I worry about being picked to be an adopting father.

Some of the couples we saw in January were still on the Agency's websites. In fact, some of the poor souls were still there months after our adventure had ended. I noticed one of them already had children and I did not feel so bad for them. Not that I thought they would be bad parents or did not deserve the chance to raise more children, but … give some of us who do not/cannot have kids a chance, eh? Is that bad of me to think that?

By now it was Friday, June 12, 2009. On the day before, our adoption agency/firm/thingie finally received the FBI clearance sent off in February.

We need to have our finger prints taken for an FBI clearance annually until we adopt. The proper citizen of today may be the Bolshevik anarchist of tomorrow. But for this year we have proved we are Americans loyal and true. If we only had a baby with which to wrap in our flag.

I drove to work that Friday; at that time a 50-mile-one-way trip. I worried about the traffic. I worried about getting home that night in time to clean up the house for our game session with friends – this was the same core group of gamers I joined years before where I met Esther.

What would the collective noun for a group of people who play role playing games be? A gygax of gamers? Nah. A tolkien of gamers? I like that better. A troll of gamers? Even better! A rule of gamers. Or better still, a reuel of gamers! Perfect!

Other than worrying, this is the kind of thing I think about while driving. What else can I do? Listen to the radio? There are only so many times I can hear "Takin' Care of Business" and "Turn the Page" without driving into a lake. I drive an old car – a 1999 Pontiac Bonneville – that still has a cassette player. It is too old for a CD player or (gasp) an MP3 player. The cassettes I carry in my car are some comfort, but they only last about ten plays before deteriorating.

So while I drive, I think. And worry.

It's already past May and the four-month deadline is coming up. We shouldn't limit our options, I decided. When I get to the office, and when I have time, I'll instant message Esther to ask her to tell Helen if there are any available children in the Lutheran or foster home system to consider us for adoption. If we decide to adopt through the state we will thank Adoption Network for their help, pay them for their time and ask them to remove us from their potential birthparent website.

Solely because of my decision, of that I firmly believe; at 11:00 am Esther called. We were selected by a birth mother to adopt her baby when it is born.

⌣⟶

*E*xcept for an email from Laura telling us about the FBI clearance, Cary has been our counselor/case worker for the past few months; and she would remain so until the frantic finale.

I had time in my schedule to talk to Cary and Esther on a conference call at noon. She told us about Valerie. She was 38 years old and has had two other children who were also given for adoption. She was a cashier at a clothing store chain in Massapequa, Long Island, New York.

The list of famous former residents of Massapequa is impressive: Jerry Seinfeld (he said Massapequa is an Indian word meaning "by the mall"), the Baldwin brothers (Alec and siblings - Alec made a joke about "not knowing

Massapequa" on a Friends episode), Ron Kovic (anti-war activist who was the subject of the Oliver Stone flick Born on the Fourth of July starring Tom Cruise - some of the movie was filmed there), Dee Snider of Twisted Sister, Peggy Noonan, pro-wrestler Taz, Joey Buttafuoco, Brian Setzer, Helen (Supergirl) Slater, Christine Jorgansen (first sex change recipient, or donor depending on your point of view), Marvin Hamlisch, Steve Guttenburg, John Gotti, and Neil Diamond!

Valerie was (and probably still is) Catholic but does not care if the child is raised in that faith. Cary told us about Valerie's parents, siblings and their children.

Valerie does not want to meet us face-to-face and does not want to see the baby when it is born. Neither does she want to know the sex of the baby (which axiomatically means that we won't either until he/she is handed to us - our minister asked if we had any legal right to know such things. I told him that except for potential future health issues - Down's syndrome, etc. - we have no legal rights at all until the baby is 72 hours old and Valerie signs the papers).

I have done only one adoption in my legal career, and that was back in 1994. I was guided through it by an associate named Julie and I remember her lessons to this day.

That Valerie does not want to see the baby or know its sex is not unusual, nor is it recommended – this is 1994 talking, keep in mind. "You never give the baby to the birthmother," Julie said. "She'll hold him; she'll kiss his forehead and never give him back."

It's cold, but that was the legal gospel back then. Julie said she has never had an adoption go through when the birthmother is given the newborn. When the baby is born, you give him to the birthparents or at least let a state caseworker put him in a foster home to await the proper legalities.

Calm down; I know this sounds like something they would do in Oceania or Barsoom, but that is the way it worked. The birthmother knew from the beginning that was what would happen, too. … didn't make it the right thing to do, though…

It became a rare thing by 2009, though. Fortunately the system lightened up and realized that the more communication there is between the birth mother and birth parents, the less draconian and heart-wrenching the transfer became.

The birthmother knows (hopefully) that she is giving the baby to a family that she has talked to, met and perhaps even befriended. That's the point of all the letters and photographs and phone calls. If she is convinced the baby will be in good hands, she can let go and be at peace.

I think that way is better, too. How Valerie or any birthmother feels after the baby is born is beyond my comprehension. I would worry about the baby every day of my life. Every day. Is she being fed and bathed and loved? What is her school like? Is she being bullied at school? How are her grades? She's not going to marry THAT doorknob, is she? She's pregnant? So soon after being married? Shouldn't they have some time to be a couple? When is she due? What hospital? What does she need?

It is Esther and my job to convince the birth-mother not to worry. We'll take care of the baby; hopefully one tenth as well as the birth-mother would.

So Valerie did not want to see the baby or meet us. It made sense to me, even though it was old and out-dated reasoning.

This was her third child – so she has gone through this twice before. Maybe she tried the "open" technique and didn't like it. Maybe she did the "closed" method and was satisfied.

I'll never know; but it was her decision and I respect it. A stiff upper lip can only last so long. If seeing the baby would make her resolve crumble to dust; I don't blame her for that.

The father's name is Jonathan and he is a taxi driver.

The child will be Caucasian. From the beginning Esther and I said we were only concerned about raising an African-American child in a potentially hostile school environment and had no other restrictions on the child's nationality. But I was glad Cary told us so that we knew before the baby was born.

Cary told us the baby's due date is September 23rd.

Esther said it was a sign the baby was meant to be ours.

Why? Because September 23rd is a very special day...

September 23rd is the birthday of Ray Charles, Bruce Springsteen, Mary Kay Place, Julio Iglesias, John Coltrane, Mickey Rooney, Caesar Augustus and Walter Pidgeon. Saudi Arabia was made an independent state on that day. The Keystone Cops released their first movie. Professional baseball was "born" (the New York Knickerbockers adopted their rules code — the first baseball club to do so). Neptune was discovered. Nixon made his "Checkers" speech.

September 23rd is my father's birthday. It is my nephew's birthday.

It is the date Esther and I got married in 2000.

This was meant to be.

"So do you think you might be interested," Cary said.

"Well, we were going out to dinner tonight anyway," I said, "we can talk about it and let you know by email tonight."

"Oh," Cary said. She had hesitation in her voice. "No, I need to know now whether we have a match. We shouldn't wait."

"I see," I said, "What do you think Esther?"

"eee…eee…{whimper}." Esther said.

"I'll take that as a yes," I said.

*V*alerie's list of demands was small – she wanted a pre-paid gift card from Wal-Mart to buy maternity clothes.

That was another worry. Part of the deal of being selected by a birth-mother included paying for expenses.

Esther calls it "catastrophizing" – I expect the worst. The absolute, bottom-line worst. And adoptions stories are filled with the worst.

What if we ended up adopting both the baby and her mother? "I want a vacation to Aruba. I want front row tickets to see the Jonas Brothers."

Remember the Jonas Brothers? At that time they were the Beatles of the tween set back then. Sort of the Justin Bieber of their day.

Remember Justin Bieber? Right now he is the Beatles of the tween set. Sort of the Jonas Brothers of his day.

Of course, if they were like the Beatles, I wouldn't have to ask if you remember them, would I?

(Ok, Mike, stop being snarky.)

In our initial interview I mentioned this scenario to our caseworker with Adoption Network Law Center. She told me to relax – some costs are reasonable and expected; others are not. Clothing, food, medical expenses; those are reasonable. Rent and utilities? Those are reasonable too. Jonas Brother tickets? Not reasonable.

Valerie lived with her parents. She received public aid, so her medical expenses were paid by the citizens of New York. As far as I know, she didn't even like the Jonas Brothers.

We were lucky.

We sent her the gift card along with a "thinking of you" Hallmark-y card. She only wanted fifty dollars, we doubled that. In fact we sent three such cards during the course of the adoption.

Cary arranged a telephone conference with Valerie on June 17, 2009 with all four of us – Esther and I were at work. She didn't want to meet us face-to-face, but a "meeting" is more or less required.

It was slow and awkward but Cary kept the questions going — "tell each other about your family, holidays, growing up", etc.

When Cary asked Valerie if she had some questions she said yes. She had written a few out. I only remember two question vividly: "What would you do if she brought home a date and the guy was a complete jerk?"

Esther handled that one quite well – we hope to raise her with enough self-confidence and self-respect that she would not. If she really liked someone enough to bring home to meet us odds are we will like them too.

She also asked if we had a name for the baby. Yes, Arthur Michael for a boy and Abigail Maryjean for a girl. She liked those names. She said when the baby was born she would use those names rather than just "Baby Girl" or "Baby Boy".

I liked that. The baby will have always been known as Abigail (or Arthur). When the inevitable "what was my real name" is asked, we can truthfully say, "it has always been Abigail, you have always been our Abigail."

She and the father of the baby have been dating about a year. We were told not to dwell too much on him, and the information we got was already known: name and occupation.

Valerie asked us about the photo from Clyde and Virginia's "wedding". She also likes renaissance-era music and fiction and asked how often we dressed up and went to events like that.

We explained that photo was from a wedding, but we did like to go to Renaissance Fairs. Her brother Jesse Linder (aka "Jock Stewart") performs at Fairs all over the country – Bristol, St. Louis, Kansas City, Iowa, Michigan and Florida. He is in a group called "Three Pints Gone" who won Renaissance Magazine's musical group of the year in 2009. They also won the Renaissance Festival Award for Best Renaissance Podcast. I'll stop bragging about my brother-in-law, if only because I am tired of misspelling renaissance. Thank you spell-check.

Valerie loved the photo. It was what attracted her to us, what caught her eye and why she picked us.

She picked us based on that older photo – the one the rules said we weren't supposed to use.

We were lucky.

I told her we both liked genealogy and hunting down our ancestors. I asked if she knew where her family came from. She is mainly Italian, she said, but also has some English, Russian and Polish in her family history. She told us Jonathan, the birth father, is Jewish. But other than that she does not know his family history. He is also thrilled about the adoption.

I was thrilled to hear the baby would have a Jewish heritage. "But will she really? I mean she's only half Jewish." I told Esther.

"Jesus was half Jewish," Esther said.

"Yes, but only on his mother's side," I said.

She slapped my arm. "Jewish status passes through the mother's side, not the father's," Esther said. She went to school for this stuff, you know.

I conferred with some of my friends. Dawn, at that time married to my friend Neil (whom I have known since the mid-1960s), said not to worry. Yes, orthodoxy says that is passes through the mother's side, but reformers do not consider that binding. She used words like halakha and yuhasin. But the bottom line was if we wanted to consider her Jewish, some – some, mind you – of the faith would not take offense.

We were not planning on raising the baby Jewish, but we want her to know her heritage. We spent the next several months studying the traditions and holidays – Passover, Hanukah and Rosh Hashanah along with all the others. We even thought members of our church might be interested too.

To us, there's nothing wrong with Christians celebrating Jewish holidays.

If you are in a library or a book store (if there are any left by that time) and you hear someone shouting, "What!?" followed by the rending of garments, you know that either an orthodox Christian or Jew has just read the previous paragraph.

Don't try to look for them – it will only feed the scene. It's easy to tell which religion the offended person is without looking; very easy if it is a weekend. Saturday – Christian; Sunday – Jew. Orthodox version of blue laws, you know.

Otherwise the only other way to know their religion is if the rending is followed by the same person shouting, "Jesus!" This pegs him as a Christian as opposed to an Orthodox Jew. Pretty obvious as to why …

There may be other people shouting "Jesus" in the bookstore, however. Someone may be looking at the prices at the coffee shop near the entrance for example.

How do you know this person shouting "Jesus" is an orthodox Christian? (This is with a little "o" – not Eastern, Oriental or Armenian Orthodox…). Easy: the more conservative or orthodox a Christian church member is, the more syllables it takes to pronounce Jesus' name. The most I've found is six. It's an easy way to determine what type of church it is:

Jesus: could be any type of church, any denomination. Probably safe to attend.

Jay-yee-sus: fairly conservative, but might allow people who are slightly different from them to attend their church, though they can't join.

Jay-yee-sus-uh: At this church there are lots of shills pretending to be healed. Oh and keep a hand on your wallet.

Jay-yee-yee-sus-uh: no gays allowed. Mixed-race couples will be whispered about behind their backs. They heal, too. Also, they pretend to blather nonsensically in tongues.

Jay-yee-yee-sus-uh-suh: healing, tongues, bring your own snake.

Anyway, the statement that caused this book to go into the "burn" pile – there's nothing wrong with Christians celebrating Jewish holidays. Jesus never forbade it. He celebrated Passover (… suddenly Last Supper …) and Hanukah (John 10:22).

So we can celebrate and teach our child about her heritage; and all three of us (and anyone else who wishes to participate – we expect our minister would be very interested in having a typical Hanukah or Passover meal) will learn about another culture and be enriched by the diversity. Where's the harm in that?

"Jay-yee-yee-sus-uh-suh…" {rend rend rend}

We asked Valerie if she would like pictures of us and our families. "Yes." We asked if we could have pictures of her. She said yes, but the caseworker later said not to expect them nor remind her of it when we don't get them.

She wrote poetry and asked if I wrote poetry. I told her I tried writing poetry, but when I wasn't writing fiction, I wrote songs.

I had been writing songs since I was a child. Mostly silly things or parodies of current songs – Weird Al became a millionaire and I became the class clown. How fair is that? But around 1981 I started writing "real" songs – verse, chorus, verse, chorus, middle eight, verse, chorus. Arena rock tunes, ballads, protest songs, story songs; all in the rock vein. I still play them – one I morphed into a pretty nice jazz tune.

Valerie wanted to see some of my songs, since it was kind of like poetry.

The days following were a massive search of the house for my songs with no results! I remember the folder where they were kept – it was a red Trapper Keeper – but it wasn't on any book shelves or in a guitar case. Where were they?

So I had to re-write what I could remember. I found some tunes written while I was in Law School from 1989 to 1992 in a small notepad among my law books. This was tucked away with my doodles and cartoons done in lieu of paying attention in class. So I sent them with a promise to send more when they were found.

My earlier songs must either be buried deeply or I threw them out, which is not likely. To compensate, I sent not only all the songs that I could remember re-written (I didn't bother with the chord progressions) but also some of my less weird fiction. We also included pages of photos printed on typing paper with captions on the back. "These are Mike's sisters." "This is Esther's mom and dad dressed for Rendezvous at Fort Massac (they dressed up in ancient garb too)".

Side note: When the baby was two-and-a-half we moved into a new house and I found the rest of my songs. They were in the bottom of a tub of our Halloween decorations. That tub had been unopened since our early marriage. Why I put them there ...

Talking to Valerie like having a stray cat in your back yard. You walk slowly toward it speaking in a quiet soothing voice, hoping it doesn't bolt away. Can you imagine it: "I picked you but since hearing your voices I changed my mind." Or "that wasn't a funny joke, the deal is off!"

Fortunately she did laugh at a few of my stories.

Esther felt more confident after talking to her and I felt worse. She was so nice! I would have felt better if she were strange or obnoxious.

Although our caseworker says this is a "98%" go, there is always the possibility she could change her mind (or something could physically happen to the baby – even though it's already six months along...). She has already dealt with the emotional effect of giving children for adoption — which is a relief, to be honest; since she has done this before she is not likely to change her mind.

We have her cell phone number and were instructed by our caseworker to call her once a week. Didn't she say she did not want to meet us? Yet we were to call her once a week?

Esther kept up that schedule – usually calling her on a Friday. By the time I got home from work it would have been too late to call (Valerie was an hour ahead of us).

It worked out well, despite that idle chit-chat isn't Esther's thing. Cary told us that was the recommended caliber of conversation.

Ironically, I excel at idle and trivial banter! But if talked to her alone ... Well, that would be awkward.

We called her together twice. Valerie was as sweet and fun to talk to as she was the first time. Nothing too important – weather and work. Kind of like talking to the spouse of a co-worker at a company party - we were passing the time with a perfect stranger.

Just before the July 4th weekend Esther gave the birthmother a call. I was on my hour-long drive home and wasn't able to chat. This time Esther got to talk to the birthfather Jonathan. They only chatted about the weather, but we both thought it was a rarity to speak with him. We wondered if we would ever hear from him again.

*A*fter the baby is born her only future requirements are pictures at 3, 6, 9, and 12 months and thereafter Halloween and Christmas photos until she is 18. I'm not sure about convincing a 17-year-old to dress up for Halloween, though, but by gum dress up he or she will.

This seemed forced. I wonder if her caseworker had to convince her to do that. Since she did not want to see the baby or meet us, wanting holiday photos seemed out of place. I can imagine the conversation:

Valerie: "I don't want anything."

Caseworker: "They are supposed to pay for your expenses, isn't there anything you want?"

"Well, maybe some maternity clothes."

"A Wal-Mart gift card it is. Now, after the baby is born; do you want them to arrange visits during holidays?"

"No, I don't want to see the baby."

"But as she grows? How about photos. They could mail you photos."

"No, I…"

"There's no harm in looking at photos. Birthday photos? School photos once a year?"

"No…"

"What are your favorite holidays? Do you like Halloween?"

"Yes." (Valerie seemed to me to be the kind to very much enjoy Halloween).

"Christmas?"

"Yes…"

"Then how about this: they send you photos every three months until the baby is one year old, then they can send you Halloween and Christmas pictures. Would you like that?"

"Sure, sure." Anything to get this conversation over with …

"Oh good."

We arranged to have a private website that Valerie, Jonathan, our lawyers and our caseworkers can access. Valerie can view all the Christmas, Halloween, birthday and any other photographs she wants.

⁓

*N*ow we worry about getting to Long Island on very short notice and staying there for up to two weeks. My aunt had some distant cousins from Long Island, but we were unable to find out their names or addresses. I have some friends in New Jersey and they were willing to help if they could. Esther's sister and husband and their kids live in Maine. That is only a little less farther than my New Jersey friends. They would help in a real emergency, but not in smaller ways. It's more likely we'd need the smaller non-emergency help - "I'm lost!"

We checked websites for possible places to stay. Most temporary apartments are meant for those with corporate accounts and are either prohibitively expensive for common folk or have minimum stays of three months or more.

The affordable apartments looked scummy (there was a computer "tour" of one apartment that cost $500/week) and the cheaper one available ($250/week) was only 300 square feet! I've been in bigger shower stalls! We decided to look into chains such as Extended Stay or Microtel.

Esther was concerned about booking motels and flights around September 23rd.

I was convinced that, barring a premature birth, if a doctor says the baby will be born September 23rd then by gum it'll be born September 23rd and only a difficult par three will convince a doctor otherwise!

We may not need to be there the entire two weeks, so unless we can get a way home earlier than planned we will spend time in the motel bonding.

I knew we would be near Oyster Bay and we might be able to see the Theodore Roosevelt sights. It might be our only chance.

Travelling back? We don't want to take a new-born on a plane (neither do the people we would sit around, I am sure) and the airlines bar babies less than two weeks old anyway. So it's either take the train or drive. Most car-rental companies frown on one-way and ... well we'd have to drive a thousand miles from New York. With a newborn. I guess we could pretend to be Apollo 11 — same cramped space for the same amount of time! And you can't tell me that Neil Armstrong, Buzz Aldrin, and Michael Collins didn't cry like babies and smell like poop during the trip! (I kid - they were consummate professionals and brave heroes!).

Fortunately, 1-80 goes all the way to Long Island and we can swing south at Chicago (or hit 1-70 in Ohio). So there won't be a lot of interstate switching! Unfortunately, Esther did some price-checking and one-way travel is so discouraged that it is priced sky high!

A train from NY to Centralia, IL (going to Washington DC then Chicago then Centralia) is expensive, but not as expensive as I had thought — plus meals are included. Esther decided to take the train from New York to St. Louis. A Chicago-Centralia trip had an eight-hour layover and the St. Louis train has only a four-hour layover. We could book a full bedroom with its own bath and it will cost only a little more than renting a car, paying for gas, one or two nights at a motel, meals, etc.

Plus, seventeen hours overnight on a train gives me plenty of time to solve the inevitable murder mystery! Unless television and movies have lied to me, all long train trips involve a murder mystery. All I need to do is hang out with either a Belgian detective or a big dumb dog and four meddling kids!

My Facebook post from June 27, 2009: "Esther spoke with the New York adoption attorney and all is still going well. Adoption law is the only area of the law where you feel BETTER after talking to an attorney..."

Esther spoke with him throughout the process – sending him papers, emailing procedural questions, etc. I only met him once in the hospital after the baby was born. He was very pleasant to deal with and knew what he was doing.

I felt awful – I had promised Esther I would take care of the paperwork for the adoption. I told her how I felt and she said she did not mind. I laid the foundation and she was more or less taking care of the little things – contacts, phone calls and emails. I have a feeling that since it appeared to be succeeding, unlike the infertility treatments, she didn't mind the work as much.

By early July we had convinced ourselves that we were going to have a baby in late September – the birth mother was satisfied with us, we were satisfied with the arrangements, the agency and the attorneys were confident it would go through with little trouble.

This was going to happen.

Oh god … I'm going to be sick.

Four

GETTING READY

I thought of the song "Soliloquy" from Carousel: I got to get ready! We let the family know first. Our fathers and siblings knew we were adopting (or trying to adopt) from the beginning. The news trickled through to our aunts, uncles and cousins. Now we announced we had been selected.

The weekend after Valerie's selection we attended the wedding of my cousin's son. It was a rare comfortable and beautiful summer day for their outdoor wedding. We did not want to take attention away from the bride and groom, but when one of my cousins asked how far along the adoption process was moving, we let them know we had been picked. Word spread and we received congratulations even from the bride and groom.

They would have their own son in a little over a year. My cousin (the groom's mother) became a first-time grandmother at the time I became a first-time father.

An aside: in my extended family there are 33 years between the oldest cousin and the youngest cousin (my youngest sister) among the original seven Curry brothers and sisters. Within two years of Abby's birth two of my cousins became grandparents and my cousin Bob became a great-grandfather. Plus my sister had another baby (her fourth – a daughter after having three sons). We have a nursery at our reunions. Abby is in the middle among her cousins, second cousins and second cousins once (and thrice) removed.

Another cousin has four children also all under ten years old (plus one that is grown and has a child; pretty common in my family – I was an uncle when I was six years old). During family Christmas parties there are up to ten children running amuck at any given time. A common call during our reunions is "You don't have to take your own kids home, just as long as you take as many as you came in with!"

In our letter to prospective birth parents, we said the child will have seven cousins and second-cousins to play with. The family has added four more since!

We received clothes from family members and friends. My sister Robin lent us her crib and changing table. The crib was a huge wooden affair with a side that drops down for easy access to the baby. She bought it in 1994 for her first baby and used it for her next two children.

The side of the crib slides down so we can gently lay the baby onto her mattress. Not much of an issue for we tall types, but Esther, at 5'3", could not reach the mattress from the raised side of the crib. It was convenient, handy and easy to use.

So naturally it had been recalled. The drop down side of the crib sometimes dropped of its own volition and onto baby's head. We decided to keep it anyway – my sister used it on three children without guillotining any of them.

How unimaginably sad for the families that did suffer an injury (or death) due to this feature.

We also bought a baby sling. These are very neat devises for carrying a baby. It fits in front while baby snuggles on your shoulder or upper chest and down and across the stomach. The baby feels like she is back in the mother's belly and you have two arms free for carrying groceries, luggage or, if on a train, pushing against the wall to keep people shoving me (and the baby) into it as they passed. It was convenient, handy and easy to use.

Naturally they have since recalled the sling, too.

The sling's brand was Infantino – they make all kinds of baby stuff. I was tickled at the name. Carmine Infantino was the editor/publisher at DC Comics for most of my fandom. He drew the Flash, Batman and was the main artist for Marvel's "Star Wars" comic among many others. He created Batgirl.

Very appropriate, the name of the company. This nerd-boy couldn't stop giggling about it. I hoped they would make Dick Giordano pacifiers and Paul Levitz diapers, too. Google their names - I'm being very dweeby here...

So we practiced the sling with Esther's old Suzie dolls and our cats. One in particular, Nebula, liked the sling. But she always liked to be held anyway. The other cats didn't stay in the sling very long before jumping out.

Hey, we cleaned the sling out afterwards! We'd risk a beheading with our Marie-Antoinette-crib but allergies due to cat dander? No way...

⟶

In my pre-teen years my mother tried to get me into stamp collecting. She bought me a few books that came with bags of old stamps to paste inside. My sister gave me stamps she received from her pen pal in England. Other family members and friends gave me stamps from Indonesia, Canada and Taiwan.

But the hobby never caught on with me. I tried coins some years later and that was more fun – especially old Roman-era coins. I still have them and will probably take up that hobby in my dotage. Through the years I tried making models; and although I enjoyed painting and putting model boats and planes together (and sometimes monsters and superheroes), it didn't take hold either.

I admire anyone into stamp collecting (or coins or model-making for that matter); it's a fun hobby and the post office makes it easy. Every few years they come out with new, fun stamps.

When I was a kid it seemed most stamps either had plants, animals, flags, hobbies, holidays or long-dead presidents, other founding fathers or esteemed men (rarely women) of history. I may be wrong here, but only as I got older did the USPS start making stamps honoring ... well ... pop culture; as opposed to cultured culture.

The first one I remember is the Elvis stamp – remember voting for the early Elvis or the later fat Elvis? The lean early king won out. Other musicians followed, then movie stars, and then TV stars! People I "knew" and recognized were on stamps!

Comic strips were next – Dick Tracy, Flash Gordon and Dagwood on a stamp! Later stamps featured Garfield and Charlie Brown.

In 2006 superheroes from DC Comics were featured. Marvel characters (Spider-Man, the X-Men, the Avengers, etc.) came later. There they were – Superman, Batman, Wonder Woman and some obscure (to the general public) characters too – Hawkman, Supergirl, Plastic Man and Green Arrow (no, his super power was not to help traffic turn left).

The stamps featured art from the various comics in which the characters appeared. So here were stamps with art by Jack Kirby, the aforementioned Carmine Infantino, Joe Kubert, Neal Adams and others! Joe Kubert's art on a stamp! The artists weren't named – heaven forfend they get recognition for their work – but I knew who drew what.

They also had Aquaman. Although not my absolute favorite (that would go to Green Lantern), Aquaman is near the top, if only because of his real name – Arthur Curry (remember?). They had an Aquaman stamp – it was a variation of the cover of Aquaman #59 (I wear the label of "nerd" like a badge of honor) and featured art by Jim Aparo.

Jim Aparo is my favorite comic book artist. I love Gil Kane, both Romitas, both Buscemas, two generations of Kuberts, Neal Adams, Michael Golden, Rich Buckler, Don Newton, Jose Luis-Garcia-Lopez (great artist, plus I loved saying his name really fast), Dick Dillon (yes I liked Dick Dillon! Sorry – that was for to the older comic book readers out there). But Aparo's art was it for me. And now his work is immortalized on a stamp!

Aparo started at Charleton Comics, where he worked on the Phantom and Nightshade, among others. He took over the Aquaman comic from the just-as-wonderful Nick Cardy. He replaced Nick Cardy (again) in another comic book called "The Brave and the Bold". Here he achieved his hall-of-fame status for his renditions of Batman.

His style is more like Neal Adams than Nick Cardy – although his first few issues of "B&B" were Cardy-esque – whose Batman was beefier and stouter like a 1950s and 1960s body builder.

Aparo's lean and lithe Batman evolved and developed quickly. While not the photographer that Neal Adams seems to be; Aparo's art is just as good – characters are alive – skinny, fat, curly hair, balding, every illustration is … well … different! Angry characters are livid, happy characters are ecstatic, surprised characters are in shock! When Batman lands a haymaker on the bad guys, the comic shudders! Aparo's portrayal of emotion and action were perfect. Aparo's Batman would be the template for the next twenty years.

The Post Office not only sells stamps and shipping material, they also sell merchandise related to their stamps. I find nothing wrong with that – it makes them money. Plus the things they sell are well-made, although expensive. Glass tumblers, posters, photo albums – all adorned with the various stamps issued. The DC superheroes were no exception. I bought a mounted poster of the Superman stamp.

They also released replicas of the stamps on postcards. While deciding on decorating the baby room (there, you were hoping this would lead to the baby eventually, weren't you?) I found the Aquaman stamp with the Jim Aparo art on a 3x5 postcard on ebay. It was batched with other postcards featuring the other DC stamps. I wanted the Aquaman one!

"Sweetie, I have an idea," I said to Esther. "We can do a nautical theme. I can get this postcard and set up a little Aquaman theme on a shelf – I can get my Mego action figure, maybe an issue or two of one of his comics and this card!"

This was when she told me that underwater themes cause asthma. I still can't quite wrap my mind around that, but we agreed no underwater theme. Nautical (ships, wheels, nets, shells)? Probably too much for a baby. We wanted something more serene and neutral for either sex.

So anything Disney, Sesame Street, Dora, Thomas, Bob the Builder – those were out. They would probably come later, but for now … no. In the early 1990s, my sister decided on Classic Winnie the Pooh (as opposed to the Disney version) for her first child. I liked that – very serene – and the wallpaper and characters were cute. We decided to find something similar.

Esther saw a light switch cover on ebay with a Peter Rabbit theme. Cute bunnies dressed in blue jackets standing amid green and yellow grass. The colors were pastel – just like any and every color in the late 1980s (remember when cars were the color of Easter eggs?). So we decided to make the baby room Beatrix Potter-themed. Esther found wallpaper, curtains and quilt patches on ebay, all with pretty, muted colors and drawings.

While traveling in Florida, Esther's father and step-mother found some Beatrix Potter prints at an antique mall. They called and asked if they could get them for the baby room. The prints were made to last and were very pretty. They fit the room perfectly.

We found large cut-outs of carrots and lettuce, as well as cardboard cut-outs of Benjamin Bunny, Jemima Puddleduck and Peter Rabbit.

If you remember, in order to adopt in Illinois we had to become foster parents. One of the requirements was that we had to have enough space in our house to accommodate the little one. We were required to have forty square feet dedicated to the baby – about the size of my office closet.

Our house had three bedrooms (we have moved since then) and we dedicated the smallest as the baby room. It was about ten-foot-by-ten-foot, one window facing south; the door led to the upstairs hallway and it had a nine-foot-square closet. The ceiling and top half of the walls were white and the bottom half of the walls were rose-colored peppered with small white dots. Strange, but pretty. A chair rail lined the room – it was the only room in the house with a chair rail.

It took Esther three weeks of stripping, priming and painting to redecorate the bedroom. She painted the ceiling and upper walls a pastel green and she put up cream-colored wallpaper with dark green criss-cross checks on the bottom half. It was very pretty and made the room much brighter. I was very proud of the job she did.

Esther loves fixing things and building things – reupholstering chairs, repairing rips and tears in curtains and chairs, varnishing and painting. You name it. She installed hardwood floors in the basement – and did a great job despite my help.

Me? I'm useless at that sort of thing. Before I was married I once walked into one of the big box hardware chains to buy a hammer. After thirty minutes or so an employee asked, "Can I help you find something?"

"I'm looking for a hammer."

"What will you be doing with it?"

"Umm, hammering … things."

So we walked half a city block to the racks of hammers. He picked up one the size of my head. "Who am I, Thor?" I said and selected a smaller one. "This will do, thank you."

I don't watch home repair shows. Now there are sixty cable channels dedicated to home repair, but before that there were some shows on PBS and one or two syndicated programs.

Before Esther, my roommates in college and elsewhen loved to watch repair shows. *This Old House, Bob Vila's Home Again*, etc. Personally, I liked *Home Time*.

Dean Johnson may have been the star of the show, but my attention was on his co-host Joann Liebeler. What a babe. When my friends and I would opine about our ideal mate (usually after having a few drinks), I said, "I want a woman like Joann Liebeler – she's smart, cute and can fix shit around the house."

When I was finally on my own, not dependent on roommates to help make ends meet, I stopped watching repair shows. I did not know Joann left *Home Time* and has had her own show. A few shows, for that matter. We don't watch those – Esther tends more to *Holmes on Homes*. I just read or troll websites on my laptop while they are on.

By July of 2009 we stood in each other's arms, basking in the warm glow of the baby's room. It captured the feel of a soft morning with greens, yellows and whites.

Esther did a beautiful job. My little Joann Liebeler.

"But ..." I said.

"What?" She said.

"Can we still have the Aquaman shelf?" I had by now bought the Aquaman postcard – I wanted it anyway (it also came with a Jack Kirby-Green Arrow card and a Neal Adams-Green Lantern card – which I have since gotten autographed by the man himself. Neal Adams, not Green Lantern...) and showed Esther what I had in mind. The Mego action figure, the comic book I was going to use. Maybe a few sea shells and a toy seahorse...

"Sure we can. Arthur will love it!"

I received the postcards in the mail. They were in perfect condition.

The next day, Valerie told us she was having a girl.

I was at my office when Esther instant-messaged me through Yahoo. "I heard from Valerie a few minutes ago" she wrote. Her weekly conversation with Valerie was scheduled for later that day, so that did not surprise me.

"She said to ask Michael how he will react to all those boys asking his daughter out on dates."

A girl? We were going to have a baby girl? I bolted out of my office to tell the staff. Ever since we got married and started planning a family I told anyone willing to listen that I wanted a girl first, then a boy. I figured the son would be too much like me and I would end up hating the little bastard. On the other hand, I was a completely enamored to the idea of fathering a sweet, little, dress-wearing, "daddy-would-you-come-to-my-tea-party" angel.

So my shelf in honor of Arthur Curry was … well … shelved. In its place were a cookie jar shaped like a head of lettuce and small, plush Peter Rabbit dolls. I had to admit it looked much better in the baby's room than my bright four-color tribute. Aw well.

A little girl!!

But I wanted a son, too.

That is, I wanted a daughter, until I discovered I was going to have a daughter. I would have been disappointed if it were going to be a boy. I know I would have. Wouldn't I?

My little baby girl Abigail.

But it would have been nice to have a son, too. "It's all right," Esther said consoling me, "anything you can do with a boy you can do with a girl."

"I can't teach her to pee her name in the snow."

"Except that."

She's right, of course, except for the peeing-her-name-in-the-snow thing. I can play catch with my daughter; I can teach her how to play the piano or guitar if she wants. I can play with her toy castles and dragons, zoo animals, a toy work bench with big plastic tools that light up and make noises when you hit them on the floor. I can swing her high on the swing, or cheer her on when she climbs up the slide.

Sounding like most haughty people who have never raised children, we don't want to pigeon-hole OUR child into sexual stereotypes. I think we will succeed. But still … deep deep down, do you really think there is a chance I will be saying, "You keep playing with your GI Joes, Abby. I'll be right back." Or "Is your baby doll poopy, Arthur? Want daddy to help change him?"

Am I being a complete pig here? Tell me if I am. "My son plays with baby dolls all the time," I know someone will say, "he practically runs his own daycare!" "You should see my daughter run around the house with her toy AK-47 wearing night-vision goggles. She pretended to break up an al-Qaeda cell just last week; I had to yell at her to untie the dog. Oh god what she does to that poor dog…"

That's great! I think that's wonderful, I really do. If I meet you face-to-face I will shake your hand and tell you what a wonderful job you are doing.

But I can't envision it for me, not with my kids. She will either be nerdy like me or a total jock. The typical parent's curse – she will be the total opposite of everything I do and enjoy. "Dad! You've got to come to my ball game tonight!"

"But there's a Firefly marathon on tonight."

"And don't forget tomorrow night I have Tae Kwon Do."

"But TCM is running all the Marx Brothers movies. And the next morning I'm leaving for Gen-Con. They're going to try to summon Gary Gygax's spirit through an Ouija board. Gygax, I tell you!"

Being woeful of what-might-have-been is part of my make-up. Or one of my hang-ups depending on your point of view. For a few hours I moped about not having a son. Then the thought of being a father to a little girl shone through the gloom.

A girl. A little girl. "Hi Daddy!" "I love you, Daddy." "Will you play with me, Daddy?" I'm in love with her already and we haven't even met.

⌒

We wanted to get the name resolved. Esther did not mind that her parents' combined name – Sheldon – would not be used. I minded. Why use my parents' names but not hers? I asked Esther to consider Sheldon Maryjean Curry for a name, but she held firm for Abigail. I was glad she did. It's a pretty name.

Why not Abigail Sheldon Maryjean Curry? Four names? My two sisters have seven children between them and they all have four names. First name-middle name-Curry-surname. They hyphenated their surname and married names and gave their children the same hyphenated last name, you see. So why not give our daughter four names, too? Lots of famous people have four names: George Herbert Walker Bush, Queen Elizabeth the Second, Mary Mary Quite Contrary, Quarter Pounder with Cheese...

Abigail Sheldon Maryjean Curry. The name was settled. And the baby's room was finished. Now we just need the baby.

⁓

On July 27th, a week after we were told our baby was a girl, we received a copy of the sonogram through an email from the New York attorney.

"Do you see the baby?" Esther said.

"No," I said.

"There's her nose," Esther said and pointed to the computer screen.

"Next to the space shuttle?"

"And there is her mouth and her head – you can see an arm right there."

"Are you sure that's not a dolphin? Don't give me that look!"

"What look?"

"That look you're giving me right now!"

Eventually I did see her. I was looking toward the bottom of the picture while Esther pointed to the upper right. Ah, there she was! She still has that pouty profile at times.

We posted the sonogram on Facebook and showed it to anyone else who cared to look, including my staff. "Look at that little nose!" The staff (three ladies) pored over the picture.

"You can see her profile?"

"Of course, she's beautiful!"

By this time the other attorney was finished with his appointment and came to my office to see. "This is the sonogram of our baby," I said.

"Is she in the space shuttle or next to the dolphin?"

Our Facebook friends asked when the baby was due and what names we had in mind. They also asked about Esther's health. They thought she was pregnant.

Esther joined Facebook in March of 2009 because of work. Imagine joining Facebook as a job requirement... That summer she was to do a presentation on social media and started a Facebook and MySpace account. She asked me to join too. By the time I got around to it MySpace was already on the outs so it was Facebook (and later Google Plus) for me.

We started the adoption before either of us joined Facebook. It didn't take long to post pictures of our new baby room and post the sonogram. No wonder some people thought Esther was pregnant.

Facebook is a great way to keep in contact with family members and old friends. I was soon festooned with pictures of kids and pets and plates of food. I loved it. This kind of silly and inane trivia is just the kind of conversational level I enjoy. "Did you have a good trip?" "Can I see some pictures?" "I love dressing up for Halloween too!" I set up pages for class and family reunions; event pages for birthday and anniversary parties. It is a good way for our gamers group to say "I can't make it this Friday" or "I am bringing chili".

I also got contacted by people I had forgotten about or hoped never to see again. "This guy was a jerk thirty years ago, maybe he's changed. {Accept friend request} Let's go to his home page. Hmm. Nope. {Remove friend}"

I'm sure I was removed or ignored too. There are two people in particular who have never accepted my friend request – a DJ I once worked with and a friend from undergrad. I wonder if I pissed them off for some reason.

I love "friending" professionals – writers and artists whose work I admire – ranging from Michael Nesmith to Jonathan McCollough. Some have a personal account and some a "group" account – it depends on how popular they are. You are only allowed so many "friends" and if you are popular enough you fill up quickly. I have had a few writers who asked me to unfriend them so they could invite me to their "professional" page. Now they can keep their personal account for your family and close friends. I'm cool with that and do not blame them.

They announce their latest work to be released or appearances and comments about public events. Most of the responses are fawning praise. Once in a great while I make a pithy comment that they respond to or "like". That makes me smile ("She noticed! She noticed!").

I hope Facebook evolves into a kind of group email provider, despite the games and groups available. People will contact each other through Facebook the way they do now through Yahoo Messenger. My staff and I already use it to contact each other after hours – I'm sick and won't be in; don't forget to review the petition …

Just as Facebook "replaced" MySpace, who knows what someone is cooking up in their basement right now that will replace Facebook in a few years.

———

*O*h why can't I have an easy job? Not that I don't love my job – I certainly do. But sometimes I wish I worked where I knew I would have an easy, relaxed day. No pressure; no stress. I would do my work and go home satisfied at a job well done.

A manicurist at the Howard Hughes Medical Institute is what I mean.

So is being Michael Caine's script advisor. "Here's a film starring..."

"I'll do it!"

"This one has a script by..."

"I'll do it!"

"I don't think you should even read this treatment, it's pretty..."

"I'll do it!"

A weatherman in southern Illinois is another easy job: easy in that there aren't that many surprises. Oh sure you have tornadoes attacking every night during the spring; but at least that is predictable and there is some solace in that. All I would do is stand in front of a TV camera from 7:00 pm until about 2:00 am screaming, "Get to the basement! Get to the basement!! What are you people, morons!? Stop video-recording it and run like hell!!"

August would be the perfect time for that perfect job. In late July I would make several takes wearing different outfits while repeating, "Today – hot and humid with a chance of thunderstorms in the afternoon. Tomorrow – hot and humid with a chance of thunderstorms in the afternoon. Future-cast shows – hot and humid with a chance of thunderstorms in the afternoon". They could air that all month - rotating the footage so it looked like I at least changed my clothes - while I spend the next 40 days somewhere cooler; like the lower Amazon or equatorial Africa.

In August of 2009, the weather in southern Illinois consisted of showers. Baby showers.

Strange things, baby showers. You are the center of attention in every detail except for the gifts. It's like standing in for someone at their birthday party. "Oh, a yoga mat! I'm sure he'll love it."

Between us Esther and I had four baby showers. My sister Kathryn conspired with Esther's best friend Arlene for the biggest shower. It was at the local smorgasbord and plenty of family, friends and co-workers were there. The place was festooned with cards, decorations and balloons. They made candle holders shaped like teddy bears in crinoline dresses to set at each table. I enjoyed talking to some friends I had not seen in many years and catching up with family since our July reunion.

And we got quite a haul! Lots of clothing and blankets and diapers. Plenty of baby toys – rattles, plush animals, dolls and books. We got a poopy-diaper pail. Interesting invention that: the poopy diaper is shoved through a system of interlocking passages into a self-sealing bag to block the odor, allowing it to ferment at a slower pace. This means the weary parents only have to change the pail once a week instead of every thirty-five minutes.

Removing a long plastic bag filled with a week's worth of poopy diapers is akin to wrestling a hungry anaconda; and a particularly smelly anaconda. After a few tries I got used to it and in a few weeks I could wrestle the thing into the trash can with the finesse of Jim Fowler – or Steve Irwin if you're too young to get the Fowler reference; or Jack Hanna if you don't get the Irwin reference – all while Esther watches me, cuddles the baby and laughs; looking eerily like Marlin Perkins holding a martini glass. If you don't get that, ask someone who laughed at the Jim Fowler reference...

My oldest sister Yvonne got us two Bibles including a Catholic Bible. Not knowing any better, I was surprised to see some additional books in the Catholic Bible than in the more familiar (familiar to me, that is) King James Version. Since Abby's birth mother is Catholic, I thought that was nice. I read all about the Maccabees. I did not know until later that Yvonne and Emmett (my older brother) were raised Catholic (they are my half-siblings from my mother's first marriage). Mom's first husband was Catholic. I had never seen his photograph until Yvonne posted some on Facebook.

We knew about that shower - it would have been impossible to keep it a surprise for Esther and me. But Arlene and Kathryn did a great job keeping us out of the loop as far as guests and decorations.

The shower at Esther's work WAS a surprise though! They held a "staff meeting" at lunch and someone had "forgotten" their notes. They asked Esther to go get them. She thought that was a strange request and knew they wanted her out of the room for some reason. When she returned there were decorations, a cake, a banner, balloons, snacks, punch and presents waiting for her. Someone managed to take a photo of her as she walked into the meeting room. She hunched her shoulders and gave off her adorable grin. I was invited and was told not to let Esther know, but I was unable to juggle my schedule to make it (I was still driving 100 miles to and from work). I told her later I knew about it and she said she thought something was up, but I am glad they surprised her.

More clothes, toys and diapers.

Our church planned a baby shower, too. It's a very mellow church – musically, politically and in its sermons – and I adore going. The members are kind, sweet and have a good sense of humor. And they love pot-luck dinners; that appeals to the old-fashioned midwestern Presbyterian in me. I was raised to believe you could not get into heaven without bringing a covered dish.

More clothes, toys and diapers and a second poopy diaper pail. We got a "Baby's First Bible" with fairly watered-down versions of famous tales: Cain and Abel were ignored, Joseph's brothers were a bit more easy-going and they went straight from the last supper to the resurrection. Showing a Mel-Gibson-esque cross-nailing would not do in a baby book.

Come to think of it, why don't more Christmas programs include the Slaughter of the Innocents? A congregation would talk about that for years!

Esther's staff planned a baby shower for her; my staff planned a baby shower for me. We had to block the calendar off for two hours. It would be impossible to genuinely surprise me – sure as heck a client would have run long or another would have shown up with questions and the party would have had to be postponed.

"It'll be a guy-themed baby shower," one paralegal said.

"A woman in a cake?" I said.

"No."

"A pregnant woman in a cake?"

"No."

"… not a baby in a cake…"

No, thank goodness. We did have a tasty cake and drinks (colas – no alcohol during work hours) and gift cards as presents. It was very nice and a sweet thing to do. Most fathers do not get their own showers; but as seems to be the case in Esther and my relationship, marriage and now our parentage, the unusual is the norm.

More good news that August: Esther's brother got a new job — he would be working as an order-filler at an online baby clothing and supply store! He can get us a 35% discount on baby gates, clothing, etc. Sweet!

Along with the shower gifts and the 35% discount at the baby store, we bought boxes and boxes and boxes of baby clothes on ebay. Every few days I would come home to find Esther on the floor in front of a cardboard box the size of a steamer trunk folding baby clothes. Ten bucks, fifteen bucks, sometimes twenty would buy us enough clothes to satisfy the Octomom.

I had never given much thought to baby clothes. "Why are these clothes in this pile?" I said.

"Those are summer clothes for newborns. By next summer she will be too big for them. Over here are summer clothes for six-to-ten-month olds."

"What if she is too big or small for them by then?"

"I doubt that, but we'll have enough."

I sometimes wear long sleeves in the summer and short sleeves in the winter. What's the big deal? For babies it IS a big deal. I have much to learn.

⟜

*B*eing an uncle prepares you for fatherhood in the same way watching Hogan's Heroes prepares you for combat.

By August 2009 I had 12 nieces and nephews, with one more to come after Abby – not counting Esther's nieces and nephews. My first nephew, Derek, was born in 1971 (three days before my sixth birthday); he died in 1976. I have nieces and nephews in ages ranging from 39 to 3. During her toddler years I rocked Abby to sleep and patted her behind while listing her cousins. Sometimes I can make it through without falling asleep myself…

Being an uncle doesn't help you know about babies. I had only held little babies a few times, had never fed a baby and never changed a diaper.

Oh, I've played with them. Peek-a-boo and Tickle Monster were specialties. So was the game "What does an animal say?"

Me: "What does a cow say?"

Niece and/or nephew: "Moo."

"A cow doesn't say Moo, a cow says Oink Oink."

"No, that's a pig."

"A pig doesn't say Oink Oink, a pig says Ribbet Ribbet."

"No, that's a frog."

"A frog doesn't say Ribbet Ribbet, a frog says, Hi Ho Kermit the Frog here."

As a father it will be my job to teach the correct animal sounds before I can mix it up. I've never had to teach animal sounds.

We go to the zoo and see a giraffe. I tell my nieces and nephews, "that's the strangest looking cow I've ever seen."

"Oh Uncle Michael, that's a giraffe."

Someone had to teach them that was, in fact, a giraffe and not a cow. As a father, that someone is me. Where's the fun in that?

And discipline. Discipline? An uncle doesn't discipline. An uncle gets them all wound up and spins them back to their parents.

Once one of my nieces was acting up. "Yell at her to stop," my sister-the-mother said.

"Why?"

"She'll stop if you tell her to."

Ok, "Stop it!"

"Waaaaah!" said the niece.

"Waaaaah!" said the uncle. I made my little niece cry. I'll be drummed out of the Uncle Fraternity. And then damned to hell for eternity. You made a little baby girl cry, you bastard!

I'm going to be a father in less than two months! We got the house ready, now I need to get myself ready! I need to learn basic baby stuff! But how? Practical experience? Not enough time.

I'll learn about babies the way they have been doing since the time of the caveman – I'll read a book!

Most of the books I found were useless. Well, they were fine for later on, but for what I wanted and needed, they were no help. I needed to know how to change a diaper, how to feed them, how to burp them, when they sleep, why do they sleep (well, that one's fairly obvious). Esther was there to show me the basics. Plus I found three very helpful books.

Barron's "The Baby Bible", by Birgit Gebauer-Sesterhenn, Dr. Manfred Praun and consulting editor Michael Msall, M.D.; USBN-13: 978-0-7641-3796-9 was one of my favorites. Like most books of this topic, it is chronological – it starts with pregnancy, getting the house (and yourself) ready, and month-by-month chapters on how the baby is growing and developing. Each chapter ends with a quick Q&A with questions from the fretful – what sleeping position is proper for a baby? Will her crossed-eyes uncross? How can I tell if a shoe is too small? Exactly what I was looking for.

An entire chapter is dedicated to getting baby to sleep. Another is on illnesses ranging from diaper rash to colic to seizures and how to give the baby medicine.

Some chapters – although interesting – were not helpful. Much is made of breast-feeding and the few paragraphs dedicated to bottle feeding could be summed up as "don't do it". Unfortunately we did not have much choice there.

At one point in the adoption process one of the counselors asked Esther if she wanted to take hormones to make her start lactating. She said no. I would say no, too, were I asked. I have enough trouble dribbling when I pee, let alone chest milk staining my shirt. What a gross conversation, let's move on...

Another chapter shows exercises to get your body back into pre-baby shape. Again, something we won't have to worry about, but on a whim I tried them and found the exercises are yoga-like and helpful. So the exercise chapters can help me get back to my pre-pregnancy girlish figure.

These books provide milestones but tell you not to panic if the baby has not yet reached them. By now she should be sucking on her toes, by this time she should recognize your face, by now she should be asking for the keys to the Bonneville. I was disappointed that a spreadsheet app was not included. Or would that be obsessing?

As is the case with reference books you do not read it cover-to-cover. I read the chapters that most applied us and frequently dived into it throughout Abby's first year. The other parts of the book I read at leisure.

Plus it is filled with lots of photos of cute babies and their attractive mothers. The mother on page 185 and the mother demonstrating the exercises are hotties. Yes, I'm being a complete pig here. It's a father's memoir, you know.

"The Baby Bible" is readable, sensible, logical and (in hindsight) accurate. We made a good choice here – it is the best book about baby-raising I found …

… that was NOT written by Dr. Miriam Stoppard.

Dr. Miriam Stoppard is a living Hestia – my goddess of home and hearth. If I ever meet Miriam Stoppard I will bow to one knee and kiss her hand. I bought two of her books and read through them daily as if they were the Gospel of St. John.

We picked up two of her books. They were both by DK Publishing. If you see a DK book about a subject in which you are interested, get it. Each book has beautiful illustrations and simple (but not simplistic) text on any issue – traveling to Ireland, the history of Superman, and baby care.

Stoppard's "The New Parent" (ISBN: 0-7894-1997-7) has it all – development from Day One. It even splits development between boys and girls. Girls learn language faster, girls look at faces instead of objects, girls do not have penises; basic stuff I need to know as a new father.

As with all such books we skipped over the parts about pregnancy, gestation and birth. Interesting, but not relevant.

"The New Parent" also discusses the relationship between the father and mother after the child is born; what the mother wants and needs – how to talk to her and to take care of her as much as the baby. This was important and something I had not thought about. I need to learn to take care of both of my babies.

The book discusses baby cribs and strollers. It talks about breast feeding, but gives equal time to bottle feeding. This was one of the main reasons I bought the book. Measuring, temperature, cleaning, plastic versus glass – great stuff.

It also had step-by-step illustrations on how to change a diaper, how to bathe a baby, how to put a shirt on over a baby's head and how to put her legs in a sleeper. There is a chart telling me what temperature to keep her room.

Baby's have different cries for different things. Really? I thought they just … well, cried. One cry says, "I'm hungry". Another cry means, "I'm cold". Another cry means, "My father has to read a damn book to learn how to put clothes on me!"

The final pages became my favorite part of the book – a month-to-month listing of the baby's physical, mental and emotional development. I referred to it so often it was in pretty poor shape by the end of the first year. We pitched it instead of donating it to the library. I guess I could have bought a new copy to give to the library. Hadn't thought of that.

At the end the book was in awful shape; the contents were anything but…

We also bought Stoppard's "Baby's First Skills" (ISBN: 0-7566-0953). A compact version of "New Parenting" – it even had some of the same photos – it also concentrated on the month-to-month development; but this book focused on play!

It presented a "Golden Hour" of play with your baby and listed 48 things you could do. #1 - play with bubbles, #9 - play with puppets, #11… crinkly toys; singing time, snuggle time, tickle time. …Those aren't the real numbers, but you get the idea.

Each chapter represents a month of baby's life and contains a pie chart/clock. For example, in Baby's first month during the first 5 minutes of the Golden Hour you can do numbers 1, 45, 22, or 4 with baby. For the next seven minutes you can do numbers 3, 4, 18 or 23 with baby; and on through the hour. Then on to the next month. Some of the hour's activities were also done in the previous month; some are new things to do. Then the next month, then the next.

The book is a treasure for we "A"-type obsessive-compulsives. I tried to follow the book meticulously with Abigail.

Didn't work.

But I still loved playing with her and snuggling with her. As an expecting new father the book filled me with ideas on how to play and what to do with her. I loved the book; I just loved it!

I pored through every page of all three books that long summer.

The one similarity between all the books was – talk to the baby. Talk. Talk. If he or she is awake, chatter with her. Look her in the eyes and sing a song. I did that. I loved doing that, being a natural chatterbox anyway. I tried not to be too sing-songy or sweet – I don't want her to be raised speaking "baby talk". It must have worked – now we can't get her to shut up.

What about Dr. Benjamin Spock, you ask? We flipped through his books, but I only thoroughly read his last one, "The Sincere Apology".

I tease. Dr. Benjamin Spock got a lot a bad press over the decades – mostly from people who disagreed with his politics as much as his views of child-rearing. Did he create the generation of lazy hippies, as his detractors said? No, get real.

In essence he said to be natural and comfortable and, most of all, kind. He later applied that not only to babies but to every human being. Why is that wrong?

Moderate strictness and moderate permissiveness is emphasized.

But I still give Dr. Spock some grief. It's all in fun. Besides, what does a Vulcan know about raising kids anyway? Plus Sarek and Amanda really did a number on their kid – you must admit.

On Tuesday September 8th we received a call from Cary. Valerie was having stomach pains.

Def Con 2! Homeland Security Threat Level Mauve! Red Alert! Red Alert! Ah-oooga! Ah-oooga!

Stop! It's only the 8th; the baby isn't due until the 23rd. What gives?

It is possible, even likely, that Valerie will have the baby early. Why? A secretary told me her theory: I'll sound like a complete mysogynist but it was her theory, not mine. Let me put this nicely –this is Valerie's third baby. The trail has already been blazed, so to speak. Abigail will be boldly going where other babies have gone before. The tubing has been loosened a bit. Get it? Whether that has any medical merit I have no idea and I am sure I will be corrected if wrong.

But we have to be ready in case the baby is born over the weekend. By now we had websites bookmarked and knew exactly what we needed to do. If the baby was born in the next few days we could fly out of St. Louis via Southwest on Saturday the 12th. The cost was fair even at this short notice. We could reserve a car with a baby seat at the airport. We picked an Extended Stay motel in Bethpage – it was nearest the hospital and had a kitchenette and two queen-size beds. For the trip home we could take Amtrak on the week-end of the 20th. I preferred the New York-Chicago route with a bedroom, but another route – New York-Washington-Chicago was also available. Then the train from Chicago to St. Louis (a five-hour layover).

We would be home by our wedding anniversary!

An obstacle appeared that evening when we checked availabilities. I should have realized it would be impossible to make reservations at a motel in New York over a September 11th weekend. Uh-oh.

Where will we stay until Monday or Tuesday when the weekend is over? In the hospital? Will Valerie and her parents put us up? Doubtful. There's no point in going until we can secure a place to stay – the baby could be four days to a week old by the time we get there. Will she still be in the hospital? A foster home? Our little girl being held by perfect strangers? Wait, we're foster parents. Our little girl being held by people like us? I'm going to be sick! Again!

There were no close friends or relatives anywhere nearby. My Aunt Iris did have some distant cousins in that part of Long Island. If she were still alive our problems would have been solved. "I have a cousin still living there. You're going to stay with his son's family in the pool house." At the airport we'd have been met by a small shivering man holding a sign saying "Curry".

"We thank you for your hospitality," we would say, "but you don't have to put us up, we can get a motel room."

"No, stay with us. You don't understand. Do you know what will happen to me, to all of us, if Iris finds out you stayed in a motel? Oy vey iz mir …"

I have been so lucky to have had some dear and sweet aunts (and uncles). I am glad Esther got to meet Aunt Iris – they got along from the moment they met. When they meet in heaven Abigail and Aunt Iris will be inseparable

I wish Esther and Abigail would have met Aunt Marge and all my departed family.

They both love my surviving aunts and uncles. Just before turning two Abigail was able to say (very clearly) "Uncle Wayne" to his delight.

We did not need to worry after getting to New York after all. The next day we learned the stomach pains were a false alarm. Perhaps a bad burrito, I said. At least we won't have to worry about sleeping on Valerie's couch.

September 9th was the day the entire Beatle catalog was re-released on CD; all remixed, shined and polished. I posted on my Facebook wall: "False alarm on the baby front last night, but, to embrace today's Beatle hullabaloo, "It won't be long yeah yeah yeah yeah yeah yeah (their true genius in songwriting came later…).""

"*A*re you going to call her Abby?"

I was asked that a lot during the summer. Esther replied, "We'll see. She can decide her name."

"No," I said. "Everyone else can call her Abby. I'm calling her Abigail."

We thought of so many names and nicknames we could call her – Abby, Gail, Abbygirl, Babygail."

"Abby Road," Esther said.

… "y-"…

Why yes, Abby Road. I hadn't thought of it until Esther said it. Of course. I have been a Beatle fan ever since my brother Emmett gave me his record collection when he went into the Air Force. "Here," he said.

He might as well of set off a grenade for the change it made in my life. I still have those LPs.

He gave me his Red and Blue albums (the best-of compilations from 1973) and "The Beatles" (called "The White Album") from 1968. He also had "Alpha & Omega" – a bootleg four-record best-of that also contained some solo tracks. It was so successful they rushed out the Red & Blue albums to stop the financial bleeding and to keep all that money for themselves – or for whoever owned Apple Records at the time.

I loved collecting their albums. I relished hearing tracks I had not heard before – here were songs that weren't on any of the compilations albums or played on the radio. "Getting Better", "The Night Before", "For No One", "It's All Too Much", "One After 909" (for my money one of the best tunes ever; Paul McCartney said they never like that song because of the silly lyrics. Well, womp bomp a lula, a lim bam boom, imagine a great song having silly lyrics. It's rock and roll!)

As a youngster, I identified more with their earlier songs than the later experimental ones. As I got older that opinion reversed. As I got still older the pendulum swung halfway back – I enjoy the entire catalog. I even dig "Revolution 9".

I can sit through an entire showing of "Magical Mystery Tour"; I'm that big of a fan…

"Baby's in Black"? "Mr. Moonlight"? It's hard, so very hard, but I manage to enjoy them, too. Thank goodness those are only two minutes long. I usually close my eyes and think of England. Even while driving.

Abby Road. Why didn't I think of that? Abby's not such a bad nickname after all.

⌢

$\mathcal{T}$hat Thursday night (September 10th) we ate at a Chinese restaurant for dinner. Esther's fortune cookie said, "You will get a cheerful message". Mine said, "You will do something different this weekend." Sleep in a Long Island hospital emergency room, maybe?

We got message after message that next week.

Valerie continued to have stomach pains and her {clears throat} exit ramp continued to dilate. It's almost time.

It's almost time. Saturday, Sunday, Monday, Tuesday …

By Wednesday the 16th, our counselor said the baby would be born over the weekend. We had better plan on being in New York when it happened. By this time the 9-11 commemoration participants had fled and the motel we wanted had plenty of rooms available. We booked our flight for Saturday morning and our train trip back for October 1st (the NY-DC-Chicago-St. Louis route was cheaper – albeit longer - so we decided to take that way home).

I had a trial on the 23rd, but the other two attorneys at the firm said they would handle it. I continued to see clients and finished the week with a 2004 examination – that's the bankruptcy version of a deposition – on Friday afternoon.

We cancelled our Friday night game session, packed and went to bed as early as we could. Like either of us could sleep.

"But wait," you say, "weren't you told that you would not be given the baby until several days after she is born? Why are you leaving before the baby is even here?"

Good question, and one I never thought of until after I reviewed my notes for this memoir. I think we were panicked into going by the adoption facilitator (note that when I have something negative to say about it, it's a facilitator…). They convinced us, and we honestly believed, that the baby would be born over the weekend. We checked our emails and phone messages during our flight and our trip to the motel in case the baby had already been born. We were convinced we would be travelling home with our daughter the next weekend. Absolutely, 100% convinced.

Up at 3:00am on September 19th. We loaded the car and headed to metro-east St. Louis. We parked our car at a community college that had a Metro-link stop. We took up four seats and chatted through the hour-plus ride to the airport. My father would pick up our car later that morning and keep it at his house until our return. We were on our way to New York to become a family of three.

Start spreading the news, we're leaving today…

Five

A LONG WAIT ON A LONG ISLAND

Travelling and I have a love-hate relationship. I love seeing new places, going to museums, eating at local restaurants, drinking regional beers and learning about the local history.

I just hate going.

I did some research on who first said, "Getting there is half the fun". No one knows who coined it. I don't blame them for remaining anonymous.

In my experience, getting there is hell. Going back is also hell, but at least the terrain is familiar.

Whether it is being cramped in a car hoping to find a decent radio station or sitting in a cramped airplane behind an adult whose parents never taught him the meaning of "indoor voice", arriving at my destination is such a relief I usually need a few hours in the hotel to unwind (read: nap).

I've had fun trips, don't get me wrong. Twice I have taken a driving tour of Georgia – from Warm Springs to Andersonville to Stone Mountain. I and two other bachelors rented a Cadillac, got some great books on tape (cassette tapes back then) and enjoyed the drive and the company. We visited my cousin at Werner-Robbins, took a long side-trip to Gatlinburg and had a blast. "I gotta stop to pee." "Let's stop here to eat." "Strip club!!"

Well, maybe not the last one, but you get the idea. Wanna stop? We stop. If a motel was booked, or the place had an ambiance that said we might not live to see the dawn, we moved on to the motel at the next exit on the interstate.

We were on our own time and free to stop where and when we pleased. Maybe that is what they mean by "getting there is half the fun", but those cases were pretty rare.

Car travel. This is the best way to go despite its problems. It's the cheapest way to travel; and you have the most control of where and when to stop. For example – I love historical markers. I stop at every one of them. It usually contains information about someone I never heard of or an event I never knew happened. I forgot what it said ten miles later, but I learned something new at the time…

The problem with car travel is the other drivers. If I had the road to myself, there would be no complaints.

I'm in the left lane of an interstate. Ahead of me, way ahead of me, is a semi. Behind him is another car. That car will have to get in the left lane to pass the truck. If he does so now he will pass the truck, get back in his lane and I won't have to hit the brake or slow down at all. I'm getting closer. He still isn't passing the truck. Closer. He still isn't passing the truck.

If your blood pressure is rising while reading this, you understand what happens next.

"For the past 6 miles, I have been sitting behind this truck. I'd like to pass, but there's no one to cut off. Ah, here comes Curry. Perfect."

That's just the interstate. State roads? Ugh. One nice thing about being stuck behind someone going 35-miles-per-hour is that eventually the speed limit lowers to match them. Then you enter a town with a stop sign. There's no crossroad, just a stop sign.

Airplane travel. All those stand-up comedians are right, you know. How can I add to the litany of complaints made by guys in sport coats in smoky rooms saying, "What's the deal with flying?"

Get in line to have your luggage irradiated and your anal cavity inspected. Get in line to get your line ticket. Get in line to get in the airplane. Wedge yourself next to a man with pointy elbows and body odor. Drink your shot glass of Coca-cola. Eat the 6 peanuts from the sealed snack bag. Try not to sneeze on the bald head of the guy in front of you whose seat is pushed back to your chest. Wish the guy in back of you who has been talking since he sat down would have a stroke. All while hoping you don't die ablaze in a corn field.

Bus travel. It's just like an airplane only without the drink and peanuts and the fear of death. Although being ablaze in a cornfield is still a possibility – your odds of escaping safely are greater.

Train travel. I like train travel. At this point I had only traveled on the train from Carbondale (Illinois) to Chicago (also in Illinois depending on who you ask), but I always enjoyed the trips. Annoyed with the people sitting around you? Move. Go to the dining car and read. And you CAN move. You can walk – stumble really – through the train to stretch your legs. You can get something to eat – a drink and some M&Ms or even a hamburger. Oh the food costs so much even the owner of a football stadium would say "damn"; but you can still eat. Plus the few times I traveled during Christmastime and loved seeing Christmas lights far into the countryside. Very Norman Rockwell.

Ship travel. Do people travel by boat anymore? Cruise ships, yes, but I mean if I wanted to go to England could I book passage on a ship? I bet it would be cheaper to buy your own plane. I may be wrong; please let me know if I can still travel by ship. I'm sure it is very nice – I would have the freedom of movement a train allows and not just in a straight line, I would have a bed and small (probably very small) room and nice places to sit and read while the ocean swells to the horizon. I would dine with the freighter captain. Much more peaceful than a plane or bus, but would it be safer?

I could die on a ship too. Hollywood has proven that many times. It helps to have Shelly Winters as a floatation device. Personally I would rather have Kate Winslet as a floatation device.

Esther looks like Kate Winslet – they both have the same smile and same eyebrows.

With my luck I'd get Earnest Borgnine as my floatation device. Then again, he did survive "The Poseidon Adventure" and from what I heard was a very sweet man. Still, if I were going to clutch onto something for several days on the Atlantic, and Esther was unavailable, I'd take Kate Winslet.

Otherwise I would enjoy my trip by boat and hoping to see deck hands chasing the Marx Brothers.

Despite my dig at airline travel, I am indifferent as to airports. I've been in the best airports and the worst airports, according to all those online lists. Frankly, they are all the same to me. As long as I am not forced to sit next to a pile of garbage while waiting for my flight, I'm okay. I don't need a foot massage; I don't need a twenty dollar cup of coffee. No Wifi? That's why God made books. Or heaven forbid I actually talk to the person I am traveling with.

Maybe it's because I've been lucky when it comes to air travel. I've had flight delays, but no cancellation. I've had to race across O'Hare to get to my new gate when the original plane was broken and we had to take another one. A delay in San Francisco nearly made me miss my connection in Denver. But those are the exceptions rather than the rules.

Nor have I had to suffer an involuntary colonoscopy from a leering TSA agent. Quite the contrary, I found most of them to be direct and receptive of courtesy. Were they courteous and friendly? Sometimes yes, sometimes no. Especially in the afternoon. If I dealt with thousands of travelers a day I wouldn't be very chummy either. They answer questions quickly and sometimes even say "You're welcome" when I say "thank you." That's good enough for me.

It helps that I am usually at an airport at six in the morning and there are not a lot of people there. I was once the only person in line and the TSA agent let me go through his station rather than negotiate the winding line to the x-ray conveyor belt. That was very nice of him to offer that.

Esther and I were not the only people in line that Saturday morning; in fact it was packed. By the time we got through TSA and to our gate they were announcing our names on the PA for last call. We shouted to the lady closing the gate door that we were here, gave her our boarding pass and walked on the plane to the same sneers I give to late-comers. We were lucky to find two seats together.

We flew Southwest Airlines and paid extra for Business Select. This got us to the front of the line when boarding and each one free alcoholic drink. Not this time, obviously.

We made it on board and readied for our trip to Long Island, changing planes at Baltimore. All was well – despite that we were last on the plane instead of first and didn't get our two drinks. But who drinks on a plane at seven in the morning?

The two clowns seated directly ahead of us, that's who...

They were two men in their twenties roaring drunk and talking as if they were sitting in a bowling alley next to the ball return. They discussed baseball, football, hockey, then back to baseball. They asked the stewardess for drink after drink.

By the end of the two-hour flight they sucked the plane's stock dry. Imagine if this were a movie - each would be played by an obnoxious Vince Vaughn in a split-screen. That comes close. One guy had a voice very much like Vaughn's from "Wedding Crashers".

They had a three-seat row to themselves – no one sat between them. Good lord, who would want to? Maybe they did that on purpose: act as loud and obnoxious as possible and you get a row to yourself.

After an hour they eventually turned into Charlie Brown adults. "Wah-wah, wah wah-wah-wah." I leaned my head against the window to watch the world pass underneath hoping to drown them out.

It worked somewhat – the trouble was now I could hear the old man behind me.

The Describer.

For the next hour the gentleman behind me described the landscape to (presumably) his wife sitting next to him. Every few seconds a low raspy voice would sound out…

"There's a bean field."

"There's a baseball field."

"That house has a swimming pool."

"There's the Atlantic Ocean." Ah, that's what that big blue wobbly thing going to the horizon was …

We both brought paperback books to read for the trip, and Esther managed to read peacefully. I barely managed two pages.

<read read> "wah-wah-wah, wah-wah" <read read> "that must be the Potomac"

Hell. Hell, I tell you! I was never more eager to get out of a plane.

But de-boarding provided no solace. As with any airline trip, the same yahoos sitting around you in the plane also follow you through the gate and onto the terminals.

After two plus hours of boarding and flying I had to use the bathroom. Esther did too, but she said she would wait. She watched the luggage (all carry-on; we checked nothing) while I went to pee. The restroom – the last bastion for peace and quiet for a man.

Or so was the hope, until the Describer walked up to the urinal next to me.

"Urine is going through the urethra; passing the penile tip. I'm urinating now."

I finished, washed my hands, left the restroom, told Esther it was her turn, sat by my bags and wept.

⌒

Thankfully the flight from Baltimore to MacArthur Airport in Long Island was lovely and relaxing...

We had lunch at some over-priced fast food chain and went to our gate. This time we had some time to wait for our late morning flight – it may have even been after noon with the time change.

This time we were first on board with our Business Select tickets: first row with plenty of leg room. An elderly lady sat on my right and Esther on my left. Since it wasn't the first thing in the morning, I enjoyed a complementary beer as part of my Business Select ticket. I also enjoyed Esther's complementary beer. I turned to Esther and slurred, "Ya know ... wah-wah, wah wah-wah-wah..."

"Shut up."

When Esther teases me she pronounces it as "Shup" and tries not to smile. She's so cute. And no, it's not the two beers talking.

I managed to read through about half my book on this one-hour flight. I brought two with me for the plane trip – a small hardback copy of "Tau Zero" by Poul Anderson and a book of Irish folk tales. I read the folk tales on the flight. I finished it by the weekend. I thought it would take longer to read. I sure hope I can find a bookstore somewhere in New York ...

We saw the New York City skyline; then the coast of Long Island. Esther and I snapped photos from our window.

MacArthur Airport was just as nice as Baltimore's and St. Louis' – as said, I'm indifferent when it comes to airports. After another trip to the bathroom we found our car rental kiosk, leased a 2009 Pontiac G6 and headed to Bethpage and the Extended Stay Motel.

The trip was about 30 miles, but seemed longer. This is natural when you are driving in unknown territory, but the two trips back to the airport during our stay were long trips, too. Fortunately the bulk of it was on an Interstate (495).

We turned onto South Oyster Bay Road. Traffic was light until we got about four blocks from the hotel. Masses of well-dressed people were crossing the road. To my right was a large building. Ah, perhaps it was an afternoon matinee of a school play or a concert and it just finished. How suburbanly serene. I mentioned this to Esther.

"Most of the men are wearing yarmulkes."

"Well, perhaps the play was 'Fiddler on the Roof'…"

"I doubt that."

We did not know it was Rosh Hashanah. As our soon-to-be-born daughter is half Jewish, and we want her to be aware of her heritage, we will have to make note of such things.

Our motel room was simple but comfy – two queen beds, a kitchenette, a small bathroom and a view of an industrial parking lot. The parking lot had a high fence surrounding a few work trucks and two airplanes wrapped in white plastic.

It was around this time that Elton John and his partner, David Furnish, were prevented from adopting a child because the Ukrainian government said he was too old and not married. The Ukrainian word for this is "homosexual".

The Ukrainian government quickly denied it was because of his sexual orientation and said it was because Elton refused to perform "Candle in the Wind" publicly anymore.

Fortunately they were able to adopt a son named Zachary. I would love Abby to meet Zachary someday. Perhaps they'll like each other, fall in love and marry. Elton's paying for the wedding, of course. Otherwise the guests on his side will have to put up with turkey roll and baked ziti. I'm advising the families of the Beckham's, Versace's, and the royals of England and Monaco right now – you'd better know how to use a spork…

Of course I thought of Elton's adoption woes when the receptionist told us our room had two queens. That's for those who think I'm that rare case of an enlightened middle-aged male WASP. I have my complete pig moments, too.

Not being able to adopt because you are not married? Why is that a problem? At that time unmarried Angela Jolie was adding babies to her collective on a daily basis. No one seemed to mind. Then again, she's not gay.

Not being able to adopt because you are gay? That's just plain stupid.

Too old to adopt has some logic to it, I suppose.

But consider who this old fart is. Elton. John. The baby's nannies will have nannies. Mr. Dwight may not be able to handle night after night of two-hour feedings, but his personal staff can. His personal staff would out-number the Romanian army; and beat them in a fair fight.

Does this mean old people can adopt only if they are wealthy? The thought riles me.

"No one over 45 can adopt." If that is your country's rule, your children are going to miss out on some wonderful parents. There are some people over 45 who are spryer than I was at 18. That's what all the testing and inspections are for.

I got married for the first time late in life. Compared to others, I mean. I also became a first-time father late in life. Both are irreversible changes; the ending of one chapter and the beginning of another.

Elton managed it. But I'm not Elton. And you aren't me. And I am he as you are he as you are me and east is east and west is west and if you take cranberries and stew them like applesauce they taste much more like prunes than rhubarb does.

I've lost my point somewhere...

Oh yes. I knew the late night feedings would be hard. The lack of sleep will affect me physically and mentally. But I was prepared to put up with it to be as good a father as I could be.

⌒

Our room faced south.

I HATE motel rooms that face south. There is no way to completely block the windows with the curtains, so every morning the sun would glare around them. Through strategic placement of shoes and luggage I managed to press the curtains against the wall and air conditioner to block some of the garish sun. Esther doesn't mind it so much – but I need it to be dark, very dark, to sleep.

There were no emails or voice mails telling us the baby had arrived. After unpacking we pulled out our map of Long Island and found our route to the hospital – Nassau University Medical Center. We decided to drive there just in case we got the call that evening or overnight so we would be familiar with the route.

South to the Hempstead Turnpike and east to the hospital. We made mental notes of the other places we spotted – a movie theater, a grocery store and a few restaurants. We found the hospital and turned back to go to a Ground Round we spotted.

I love the Ground Round. It was one of my favorite places to eat in south county St. Louis when I lived there. It had a hunting lodge/sports motif; this one was strictly a sports bar. We had a great meal.

We stopped into a grocery store for supplies. I loaded the cart with bread, cheese, lunch meat, cans of Coke, condiments, snacks, frozen food and cans of soup. Esther was walking beside me the whole time. I asked what she wanted and she said she wasn't hungry.

"Sweetie, we're buying groceries for the week. What do you want to eat?"

She picked out a bag of potato chips. "This looks good."

"Esther, this is a snack. This is going to last you a week? We're not eating out three times a day." I didn't realize what was happening until years later: she was terrified.

In a matter of days, perhaps hours, she was going to be a mother. I'm worried about whether to buy mayonnaise or salad dressing and she's worried about being a parent, a mommy. Despite all the books and videos, all the advice from friends and family for the past eight-and-a-half years – she wasn't ready. Despite all the preparations; she wasn't prepared.

I still thought of it as a grand adventure; a great vacation. In a few days we'll be having a baby, but in the meantime … let's enjoy our remaining days as DINKs (Double Income No Kids - a very trendy anagram from the 1990s).

She hid her fear. She was and still is very brave.

But is anyone ever ready or prepared for parenthood? One of the best pieces of advice I got was from an old schoolmate and father of two: "you'll make mistakes, just enjoy your baby and do the best you can. You won't break her. She'll be fine."

At the time I did not understand why Esther was acting so stand-off-ish. We took my groceries and her chips to the motel, packed everything away and settled in for our first night.

We set up our laptops and got the wifi running. We checked our emails and I played a bit of World of Warcraft. We contacted our families and friends on Facebook and posted that we made it to Long Island safe and sound – our nerves slightly frayed but in good spirits.

The TV had basic cable. I mean basic – about 13 channels. We had all the networks, a few independents, TBS, a few sports channels and the Weather Channel. No History Channel, no MSNBC.

(Esther is an avid viewer to this day – but news and commentary isn't my thing. Give me a documentary about crustaceans anytime over people trying to shout over each other. The only thing worse than being in a pointless argument is listening to a pointless argument.)

Not good. The last network show we watched with any enthusiasm was *West Wing* and *Frazier* before that. Since then we've added *Hawaii 5-0* and *Community*, but in 2009 without the upper channels, our TV watching was going to be very limited.

But so what? By Monday latest we wouldn't have time for staring at a screen – we'd have a baby to care for.

Right?

⟨⟩

*W*e woke Sunday morning refreshed. We checked emails and voice mails. No baby yet.

When we turned off the interstate we saw some shopping areas to the north, so we headed that way. We found a Barnes & Noble and spend some time looking for books. I found a few I liked, but didn't buy any. We had lunch and went back to the motel.

Esther had homework to submit that week. She decided this quiet after-noon would be perfect to get it all done now so she would not have to worry about it when the baby comes.

So she would be on the computer all afternoon, while I would …

I would …

What?

As old as I am I still enjoy reading comic books. The current crop of four-color caped crusaders is crappy – but I've been saying that since the mid-1980s. I prefer older comics – 1970s and back. I'm proud of my collection, but there are some holes I need to fill. Issue number 85 of this title; number 134 of that title.

Comic books aren't just Batman & the X-Men; not just a few Archie di-gests in the check-out aisle. There are good things out there to read – but you have to hunt for them. And I haven't even looked into digital comics yet!

As Esther decided to spend the afternoon doing schoolwork, I checked the yellow pages and the internet for comic book stores. The closest one was fifteen miles away – Grasshoppers in Williston Park. I asked Esther if I could drive over there while she studied.

"Hmm," she thought, "four hours of uninterrupted time to do a week's worth of homework or try to do homework stuck in a motel room with Mike who has nothing to do…"

"Well, I suppose it'd be okay for you to go…" she said. If the parking lot was on our side of the motel I would have leapt out the window.

It took between forty-five minutes to an hour to get to Williston Park. It was on the same highway as the Barnes & Noble's we went to that morning, so it was an easy drive. When I got to the downtown area all highway traffic was diverted north – a town fair was blocking the entire downtown area.

I parked along the highway as close as I could to the east of downtown. It was still about ten blocks. Fortunately it was a beautiful sunny day; warm without being hot and no humidity. In southern Illinois we have about two weeks of weather like this – one week in the spring and the other in the fall. I enjoyed the walk.

The town fair was typical stuff – lots of booths of crafts and artwork, lots of kiosks selling fried batter lightly sprinkled with powdered sugar. A band played a Creedence tune then 1950s rock 'n roll. Most of the shops had clearance items outside their stores for sale. It was crowded but not annoyingly so. I moved about the main street soaking it in.

The only thing missing was Esther. She would have loved it, too. I wished she there with me – I mention this to her every time the topic comes up. Esther says she doesn't mind going to such nerdly activities with me – whether it be a convention or a comic book store – as long as there was something she could do, too. If there are flea markets or antique stores in the same area as the horror convention, she'll be there. GenCon in Indianapolis? She can go to the War Museum or visit with my sister. One of my favorite comic book stores in Fairview Heights (since moved to O'Fallon) was right next to a fabric store – I was usually done shopping before she was. Being the only man in a fabric store is unnerving. And mind-numbingly boring.

Except during the holidays when their Christmas village stuff is out.

Grasshopper was a mighty-fine store. As I looked through their graphic novels, I listened to a clerk explaining the Avengers to a lady about my age. Her son was getting into comics and enjoyed the Avengers. She had no idea where to start, so the clerk pulled out quite a few books. "Here's a good story to start off reading…" The fantastic movie notwithstanding, the comic book Avengers has a long and winding history and it would be easy for a youngster to get lost, frustrated and give up. The clerk did a great job of not giving her a book that was Part Seven of Ten. "Here's a book combining six issues that starts a new line-up and tells a complete story," he said. Does your son have a favorite? Captain America? Let's find a complete story with him in it.

Bravo. Good for you, Mister Clerk. The only complaint was you dominated the "A" section of the shelves. Well, I guess I can look elsewhere for now.

I picked up the latest issue of Thor – at that time a great series (may still be, but I dropped the book at a good stopping point) and two books combining the first forty issues or so of "The Fantastic Four" from the early 1960s. I had reprints of some of the series, but these were all in order – in black and white, which was kind of a drag. Still, it kept the cost down. Having finished my Irish folklore book that morning, these will give me something to read until we get home. I mean, the baby could have been born by the time I got back to the motel, you know? I also picked up the latest copy of "Agents of Atlas" – a great series featuring superheroes from the 1950s thrust into today's world… I'm a sucker for stuff like that.

"How are you, today?" the check-out clerk asked me when it was my turn to pay. The Avengers lady had already paid for her son's bundle and left.

"Fine, you?" I said.

"I'd rather be outside today, that's for sure," he said.

"Out there?" I pointed my head toward the door and the fair-goers.

The clerk held up his index finger. "Let me rephrase that," he said in all his Long-Island-accented glory. "I'd rather be outside, but not here."

"I understand." I paid for my books and wandered the fair for a few more minutes before the long walk to my car.

New Yorkers – at least Long Islanders – drive no more aggressively than the typical southern Illinoisan. It's still aggressive, just less stupid. They still pull out in front of you – but they then go faster than you! All my time driving in Long Island I never once had to slam on the brakes after a yahoo turned in front of me and drove twenty in a fifty-five.

When I got back Esther had just finished uploading and posting her homework; I showed her my acquisitions and we went out to eat.

Baby aside of course, this was the highlight of the "adventure": a little me-time on a gorgeous late summer/early fall Sunday afternoon driving through Long Island in a fully-insured vehicle. "I'm mergin' here! I'm mergin' here!" I fucking loved it!

⌒

ing ring}. Esther's cell phone went off at 3:00 that morning. It could only be one thing.

Jonathan called – he was taking Valerie to the hospital. This was it! Battlestations! Battlestations! We washed and got to the hospital (having already driven the route – you see? smart…) about an hour after the call.

The only part of the hospital open at 4:00 Monday morning was the ER. Esther and I were the only people there. Strike that, we were the only conscious people there. Two men were asleep on the couches. They must have been homeless or visitors or both: they weren't bleeding and they didn't seem to be waiting on anyone.

I got impatient and walked to the other rooms. After fifteen minutes a nurse (maybe a nurse, maybe not, but some kind of lady-in-scrubs) finally appeared at the window. We explained that Valerie checked in some time in the past hour – she was going to have a baby. She made a call and showed us to the elevators. Maternity was on the third floor.

I wonder what ever happened to the two men on the couch.

The waiting area of the maternity ward consisted of a faux-leather loveseat and a large sectional shaped in a right angle. There was a coffee table, lots of out-dated magazines and the omnipresent television on which someone was selling knives.

A few attendants walked through the lobby – we tried to stop as many as we could to let them know we were here for Valerie. They said they would do what they could.

Around 4:30 a man walked into the waiting area. He wore a sweatshirt and sweatpants. He was tall – taller than me and I'm 6'3". He was big – well over 300 pounds, maybe 350. He looked like a friend we knew from our old church named John. Thick glasses, salt-and-pepper hair cut short; a beard. A few teeth missing.

It was Jonathan. He asked if we were Esther and Mike and we said yes. He told us Valerie was fine and it was another false contraction. They were getting ready to send her home.

So that meant we should go home too. We thanked Jonathan and took the elevator back to the emergency room and out to our car and to the motel.

We were never supposed to meet the birth parents. I guess we were lucky Valerie wasn't leaving at that time. "I don't want to meet the adopting couple; I don't want to see the baby." We respected her wishes and wanted to honor them. Valerie must have known we were in the waiting room – some nurse or attendant must have said she had some "friends" out here waiting to hear how she was.

When the doctor or nurse told Valerie it was a false alarm, did she ask an attendant to tell us to go home? Did Jonathan say, "I'll go tell them. Don't worry." Did he describe us to her? Or did she stop him, "I don't want to know." That's silly – we sent her photos so she knew what we looked like. But if you think about it, photos don't really say much. A thousand words. How can a thousand words really capture someone's personality?

Jonathan, Esther and I were cordial and friendly – as best we could at 4:30 on a Monday morning. I hope we left a good – albeit tired – impression. We posted on Facebook that it had been a false alarm (we posted before we left that the birth mother was in labor), changed into our jammies, and went back to sleep.

On Monday we received a call from Valerie's adoption attorney. Esther took the call and did all the talking, so I am not sure exactly what was said or in what tone. "Okay, okay …" She hung up. The attorney did not yell at her but made it clear that we were not to go to the hospital until we were instructed to do so. He must not have said it nicely because Esther cried. By this point on the emotional roller coaster he may have only been curt, but it made her cry. I asked if she wanted me to call him back.

"No," she said. Probably the wise thing; I would have made it worse.

I imagine the conversation if I had called him back: "All right then," I would have said, "we won't go to the hospital until instructed to do so. But you have to understand that we were instructed to … oh that's right, we haven't been instructed in anything! The last contact we've had with anyone associated with this adoption was last Wednesday when we were bullshitted into coming here because we were told the baby would be born this weekend! I understand what it's like to have no control over your clients or your agency, but don't take it out on us. Find out who was supposed to inform us as to what to do and bark at them!"

You can make most attorneys bristle when you point out the have no control over things that they are supposed to control. It's like questioning their manhood; pointing out they have little dicks. That's why you can generally never pin them down on a direct answer (that very sentence is a case in point. It is both vague and assertive – you can "generally never"? What the hell does THAT mean?).

Esther, of course, as always, was right. Such a statement would have made us feel better but would have made the situation worse. Still, it made for a pretty sucky Monday. Esther summed up the day on her Facebook post, "…is soooo ready for the waiting to be done!"

On Tuesday we travelled south and east. We went to Massapequa, Valerie's home town. We saw all the small shops and restaurants and the huge shopping center. We drove past the clothing store at which Valerie worked. I wondered how creepy it would be to go in and look around. I wondered if Valerie was working.

Doubtful, said Esther. She is too far along in her pregnancy to be a useful employee. And yes, she said, it would be creepy.

True. What if Valerie recognized us? She had photos of us and all we had to go on was a physical description from her adoption application. Plus she was probably the only clerk who would be nine months pregnant.

Esther spotted an Olive Garden and asked if we could have lunch there. I balked. I don't dislike Olive Garden, but ... we passed by so many Italian restaurants over the past few days. Eating at Olive Garden in New York is akin to eating at a Red Lobster in Maine.

But remember – I was having an adventure; Esther was terrified. She loves Olive Garden; it would be a comfort to her. And it was not an unreasonable request. Olive Garden it was.

After lunch we went further south to Jones Beach. Being mid-week, we had the coastline to ourselves for some time. By the time we left a few other people were walking the beach. We took pictures of the surf and the birds and each other.

Naturally this was the first overcast day we had in Long Island. That's okay, though, I probably would have gotten a wicked sunburn if it were as bright and clear as it was Sunday. Summer was ending and it was getting chilly. I brought only shorts – we were only going to be here a week, remember – and no long pants. If I really needed long pants or a jacket I could have bought some.

Esther always brings coats and sweaters. She's cold-natured.

Jones Beach was relaxing and soothed the soul. Esther wrote on Facebook, "…is still waiting, but managed to have a good visit to the beach. It's always wonderful spending the day with my dearest love." Yes it is.

We went to bed expecting a long next day. It was the due date. Baby or not, it was going to be a very special day.

⌣

*N*either of us are golfers, or boaters, of fisherman (fisherpeople?) or sports-oriented at all. If you are a golfer, Long Island is the place to go. Likewise if you like to sail the sea. If you are a history buff like me, well… it's not exactly Boston. But what it lacks in quantity it makes up for in quality. No slam at Boston – it has both quality AND quantity.

Ever since Valerie picked us and we knew we were going to Long Island to get the baby I hoped we would have had a day to go to Sagamore Hill. If for no other reason that it guaranteed that we'd be in the middle of the tour when Esther would get the word that the baby was born.

agamore Hill was the home of President Theodore Roosevelt Jr. He bought the land and built the house in the early 1880s and lived there from 1885 until his death in 1919.

Theodore Roosevelt is that one guy on Mount Rushmore that isn't on any money.

TR is one of my favorite presidents, if only because his life was so fascinating. If I wrote a novel about a character whose life mirrored Roosevelt's no one would buy it. He was his own "Mary Sue" character; a pulp character in the vein of Doc Savage. It would not surprise me if someone discovered TR put on a mask and cape at night and fought crime.

He was born in the upper echelons of the New York City elite – the kind of people Thurston Howell was based on. TR's mother was a southern belle who was raised on the plantation that may have been the inspiration for Tara in "Gone with the Wind". Her brothers fought for the confederacy – sword-swinging blockade runners – and one was possibly a spy in England.

His father was a businessman both gentle and strong (the two traits go together well). He died while his son was still attending Harvard. TR called him the best man he ever knew. He respected the memory of his father so much he kept the appellation "Junior" until the day he died.

He married his college sweetheart and expected to raise his family at Sagamore Hill. Unfortunately his new bride died on the same day as his mother in their New York City home. Probably to escape the sadness, he started a cattle business in North Dakota and lived there part-time for the next several years.

It was then his legend began to take shape.

He wrote about his adventures as a cattleman – roping and herding his charges, catching rustlers, enduring the heat and cold of the badlands. He helped create the modern myth of the cowboy.

He returned to Sagamore Hill, married and started his second family. Earlier he had a taste of politics in the New York Assembly and ran, and lost, for mayor of New York. He eventually became police commissioner of the city; then Assistant Secretary of the US Navy.

He resigned that post to volunteer for the Spanish-American War and formed his own regiment – the famous Rough Riders. The charge up San Juan Hill became TR's most iconic image.

After the war he went back into politics: governor of New York, Vice President and in 1901 President of the United States. All the while living at Sagamore Hill.

It was called the Summer White House during his presidency. He would hold cabinet meetings and press conferences on the front stoop. That became pretty common for presidents after him but presidential homes before his were not used much professionally during the owner's time in office. Other than Monticello and Mount Vernon I can't name any presidential home before TR at all. I have been to Lincoln's home in Springfield, IL, but he never returned to it after leaving for Washington. He never used it as a vacation spot while in office.

After his time as president, TR went on a hunting expedition to Africa (his book "African Game Trails" is a fun read), ran for president as a third-party candidate, and explored the Amazon.

He died in his bed in 1919. Here, at Sagamore Hill.

It's a beautiful place. The lawn is manicured, sidewalks roll throughout the park; all dominated by the huge blue house. There are also out-buildings, barns, a smokehouse and a small windmill, too; but the house dominates.

On September 23rd we went to the north coast of Long Island. We stopped for breakfast at the lovely town of Oyster Bay. The signs leading to Sagamore Hill were very easy to follow and we oohed and aahed at the house when we approached. We swung around to the welcome center/gift store and bought tickets for the tour of the house. There were plenty of books; and although I was interested in buying a pith helmet they had for sale, we did not buy anything that day.

I've read the following books on TR and they are all a great way to get to know our 26th president: "The Roosevelts: An American Saga" by Peter Collier, "The Rise of Theodore Roosevelt" (this one is particularly good) and "Theodore Rex" by Edmund Morris (he has since published the third book of his trilogy), and of course "Mornings on Horseback" by David McCullough. I also have this on audio cassette and listen to it in the car once or twice per year.

Yes, my car still has an audio cassette player.

I've also read some books penned by the man himself: "An Autobiography", "African Game Trails" and "The Rough Riders". According to a friend of mine who so served in the Navy, his scholarly book on the War of 1812 is still being used as a textbook at the Naval Academy.

We were early and the first tour of the house did not start for 45 more minutes, so we walked the grounds and took pictures.

We sat on a bench and watched the caretakers mow, pick up litter, sticks and leaves; we watched a turkey cautiously walk past. It was a beautiful day – not hot, but warm enough for me to still wear shorts. I savored where I was and Esther and I held hands and basked in each other's company.

Another couple stood on the huge porch in the front of the house to wait for the tour to begin. We joined them and watched construction workers lay brick on the driveway.

The porch was huge – bigger than most living rooms. TR would use this porch for lectures and speeches. There was plenty of room up here for chairs and podiums for all the dignitaries. I stood and looked beyond to the Long Island Sound; imagining Roosevelt pontificating and banging the podium with his fist.

The words "Qui Plantavit Curabit" were carved and painted in gold over the main entrance. I think it means "bananas are good for you".

By now there were about twelve of us waiting. We were the youngest couple; one adult daughter – younger than us – toured with her parents.

The tour began at the side entrance – where the bricklayers were restoring the driveway. We were told not to speak with the bricklayers as they were busy working.

We had been talking to them for the past twenty minutes. They worked for the National Parks Service. One fellow just finished a job in Hawaii, another in South Dakota. They were replacing/repairing the brick work under the porte-cochère or coach port - a car port before there were cars…

The house looked smaller on the inside than it did on the outside. This is probably because most of the house was not accessible to the general public. But the house seemed to go up and up and up. We saw the bedrooms where the children and servants slept. We saw the bed in which TR died. We saw his study; the walls of which were lined with his trophies and memorabilia. Two feet in front of me was a glass case with his Rough Rider uniform. I gazed at it for hours, it seemed.

Dead animals lined the wall of the dining room. We viewed the seat where Edith preferred to sit while eating. It was the only place at the table where one could eat without seeing a trophy head on the wall. I could hear Roosevelt grant his wife's request to place no trophies in her line of sight while she eats; the confusion in his voice as to why she would make "a confoundedly silly request. Oh well, if she must have it that way far be it from me to argue."

An elderly gentleman had a hard time climbing the many narrow staircases and asked everyone else to go first. I did not mind and motioned him to go ahead of me – it gave me a chance to look at the many pictures on the wall and the many roped-off rooms while I waited.

Esther was even more enthralled. She loves old houses and antique furniture. She didn't want to leave.

I'm not that much into old houses and furniture unless there is some historic significance to it.

"Do you want to tour a Queen Anne-style house built in the 1880s?"

"No."

"Do you want to tour a Queen Anne-style house built in the 1880s that Teddy Roosevelt lived in?"

"Heck, yeah!! Try to keep me away!"

It was a long walk to the museum, but worth it. This was the house owned by TR's son, General Theodore Roosevelt III, a WWII veteran. His house was turned into a museum dedicated to his father.

We sat through the brief film that all museums seem to show and then on to the exhibits. Bits of clothing, letters and memorabilia under glass cases lined every room. We spent most of the afternoon there.

Just before we left, I spotted a mother and a daughter who ate lunch next to us at the Olive Garden the day before. At the restaurant the daughter talked about college and taking the train north to her school. I wasn't eavesdropping –

Esther had gone to the bathroom and I was sitting closer to the daughter than I was to my own wife. I couldn't help but listen in.

I saw them twice in as many days. I will never see them again.

⟡

I was Roosevelted out by late afternoon. We got to our car – we were in the front row and by now the parking lot was packed – and drove to our final stop planned for the day. South of Sagamore Hill was Roosevelt's gravesite. It required some climbing – sometimes pretty steep climbing – but we made it and snapped some photographs. So this makes eight presidential markers I have visited. Both Adamses (they're crypts are side-by-side), Benjamin Harrison, Truman, Coolidge, Hoover, Lincoln and now Teddy Roosevelt. I've since added Andrew Jackson. A macabre hobby true, but … it beats smoking.

We ate out before returning to our motel. Nine years ago today Esther and I became husband and wife. On this day Esther made me the happiest man on the planet. Happy Anniversary my dearest love.

Seven years ago today my nephew was born. Happy Birthday to him. I hope he had as wonderful a day as we had.

Seventy-nine years ago today day my father was born. I hope everyone wished him well. I called him that night to update him on our triumphs and travails. I think he would have loved Sagamore Hill too.

It was also the baby's due date. Esther checked her phone all through the day. No emails, no messages. No baby. Not today.

⟡

*e*sther is the Harry Potter fan of the family.

While not a fanatic, she was a big enough fan to break her rule about series books: never start a series until it is complete. I'm that way too. Whether the book is a two-parter, a trilogy, or in seven or fourteen parts; do not start it until it is complete.

If the first book sucks eggs, no harm done; you've lost nothing. Otherwise if the series draws you in, then you do not have to wait years to complete the story. Frankly, I don't have the time to remember what happened before and I won't sit through forty-plus pages of "our-story-so-far".

I am not talking about a series of books featuring the same characters – Harry Dresden, the Stainless Steel Rat, the "Myth" series. I mean the books that are one long story, or at least so dependent on the events of previous books they might as well be individual chapters of one story – like the Wheel of Time series, A Song of Fire and Ice, and Harry Potter.

I started the Wheel of Time before the series was done, but I hoped (and was proved right) that the series would be done by the time I got to the last book. I am a slow reader and it takes me over six months to slog through a WoT book. Going through chapter summations on the internet helps speed things along. Yes, I cheat and read spoilers; that kind of thing doesn't bother me.

But it is also why I haven't started reading the books based on *Game of Thrones* (A Song of Fire and Ice) by George R. R. Tolki – er – Martin. I'll wait until the end is near. I have all the books on my shelf and hear them call to me on quiet nights. "Mike … pick me up. Just read the jacket cover … now the intro … that's all … just that … then maybe the first chapter … there's nothing wrong with just reading the first chapter … join us … be one …"

Esther read the first Harry Potter book after seeing the movie. A co-worker thought she would enjoy the film and lent her the DVD. She loved it! So much so that she borrowed the book from the library. She loved that too. She broke her rule and read the next two books that were out at the time. As the later books were published, Esther would get them from the library and finish them in a matter of days. Now remember these were huge cinder-block-sized tomes that would make Robert Jordan seethe with envy!

For many years Esther's Christmas gift was guaranteed to be a Harry Potter book. I got the British versions from Amazon UK. I also got copies of the first book published in Irish, Dutch and Latin. She couldn't read them, but she loved them! One year she received the first book on CD read by Stephen Fry.

If I were president my first law would be that Stephen Fry or Edward Hermann must be the only people allowed to narrate audio books.

When she was done with it I read the first thirty pages of the first Harry Potter book, "The Philosopher's Stone" (called "Sorcerer's Stone" for us

Americans. I guess the publishers thought we needed something in the title to tell us the genre otherwise we'd think Harry was some student of Descartes or Kant. "I ain't readin' no existentialism crap, I … oh, it's about magic wands and such? Okee dokee then…").

Not knowing much about the series – what was going to happen - I stopped reading and went on to other books. Two reasons: first if I wanted to read about misopedia, I'd read Dickens. If the movies are any indication that is a very small part of the series as a whole, but it was central to the beginning of the first book. Frankly, the life of an abused unloved child is something I don't find entertaining.

"True," my friends who were big fans of the books said, "but if you would have stuck with it a little longer you would have liked it."

Maybe, but (the second reason I stopped reading that first book) I have cases full of books to read. And at that time I was reading Robert E Howard's Conan tales and his other weird fiction stories. That's about as far from Harry Potter as you can get in the fantasy genre.

I guess a better way to put it is I like a little sword with my sorcery.

Not that I dislike the Harry Potter books – how can I like or dislike what I haven't read? There was hardly a negative review for the entire run of the series. Stephen King loved them and spoke of J. K. K. Tolki- er – Rowling's masterful writing; especially in the use of back story. And if the Harry Potter series relied on anything, it was the back story. Even the back stories had back story.

Rowling could make an entire other series out of the previous events. She shouldn't, but she could. The back story was already told in the seven books. Harry Potter is basically a sequel of an unwritten epic. Star Wars was too – and look what happened when they went back and made movies of the previous events. Pee-yoo.

You have to be a good writer when using the Heroic Quest motif, oth- erwise a bad or even a fair writer will wallow in sameness. A young lad and his friends are whisked away by a strange wizard to fight the evil dark lord. Sound familiar? It's Lord of the Rings, Star Wars, the Wheel of Time, Harry Potter and countless others. The only archetype missing in Harry Potter was the seemingly-morally-ambiguous-ruffian-who-kept-his-noble-heart-and-her- itage-hidden. Think Aragorn or Al'Lan Mandragoran.

That may have been the Gary Oldman/Sirius Black character I suppose…

In the second and third Star Wars movies, I kept expecting Han Solo to be revealed as a crown prince, or whatever Lucas would have called it. "Actually, Luke, I've been in hiding all these years pretending to be a smuggler. I'm really the Gran Torino of Motrin."

The only criticisms of Harry Potter came from the same fundamentalists (emphasis on mental) that disparage anything that doesn't mention Jesus every third sentence. When Harry Potter first came into the limelight there were a lot of those on the news. One news clip showed a lady yelling at a group of children, "If Harry Potter had been around in Jesus' time he would have been burned as a witch!"

So would you, lady-teaching-in-public-and-wearing-pants. Besides, Leviticus 20:27 says witches are to be stoned not burned. Stop using your bible to thump kids on the head and try reading the thing. If you're going to be intolerant, do it right…

So I have never read the books. I did see the movies. I probably would not have seen them if Esther had not wanted to go, but I did and enjoyed the first ones.

Not being familiar with the story – back or otherwise – I was lost during the later movies. Esther always debriefed me on the way home to tell me what the heck was going on.

To me the movies went something like this: Harry went to school that year, something bad happened, Harry and friends solved the mystery and cured the badness. Along the way, Harry finds out a bit of his family history. Then we find out the evil dark Lord Voldemort was behind all the bad things. Sometime after watching the fourth or fifth movie I expected Voldemort to say "and I'd have gotten away with it too, if it weren't for you meddling kids!"

Little things bothered me throughout the movies. Some of them were resolved: why didn't Harry tell his aunt and uncle to suck it and then move into the school or with his friends (which he did).

Another problem: if all the evil wizards came from the Slytherin house, then why is there a Slytherin house? Why not break them up and dilute their evil? Like they did with Standard Oil and AT&T and the Whigs.

On Thursday September 24th we wanted something different to do. What about a movie? What was playing? Not much. Some miles east of Bethpage we found a theater playing movies from the past summer. We found the theater online and the only thing that we wanted to see was "Harry Potter and the Half-Blood Prince".

I was in a sour mood after no-baby-on-our-anniversary. So much so my Facebook post that morning quoted Lawrence Grossman, "You wait for a gem in an endless sea of blah."

Later that morning, our anticipation of the movie was made known to our Facebook friends.

Mike: "It has come to this: we are going to see an afternoon matinee of Harry Potter and the Last Temple of the Crystal Jedi, or whatever the hell it is…"

Esther: "…and Mike are going to go see the new Harry Potter movie – hopefully this will "induce" a phone call. If not, I'll finally get to see the movie."

Mike: "Oh Lord, if you are a kind and benevolent God please let us get the phone call before I have to sit through – er, rather – before we get to the theater!"

The theater was in a plaza with a Barnes & Noble and other shops. We stopped in the book store until it was time for the movie.

Esther's cell phone rang as we stepped out of the car in the theater parking lot. "It's the attorney!" Esther said. Valerie's attorney!

I stood next to the driver's side door; Esther by the passenger door with the phone on her ear. "Uh-huh…"

"Uh-huh … That's good…"

By this time I was trembling and smoke was coming out of my ears. "For god's sake provide some exposition!!"

Esther shook her head. I took this to mean no baby news. After the call Esther said he was calling to give us an update. After the Sunday night fiasco he probably decided some kind of control and oversight was needed. He was right. He was a week too late, but he was right.

"He said Valerie was feeling just fine."

"Oh goodie," I said without further comment. We were still standing beside the car.

"He said he was sorry for our extended stay, but we were going to go home with a baby."

How he knew we were at an Extended Stay I'll never know. And it wasn't a bad motel, nothing to apologize for. Oh, "extended stay" in general. I see. Well, it was nice of him to call and update us. He was very pleasant. This was to make up for barking at Esther Monday morning. It was his way of apologizing. I've had judges do that to me – going out of their way to be nice after being especially snarky earlier. Of course they chew you out in public and apologize in private. It's good to be the king, I guess...

"Twenty one dollars!?"

"That's total," said the lady in the ticket booth.

"You think I'd be more outraged if it was twenty-one each? Is Rowling going to sit next to me and narrate the damn thing!?"

Popcorn and two drinks cost even more than that. They had to have some way to pay for the mortgage on the theater. The place was immense! The auditorium was the size of a small baseball park. The chairs were larger and more comfortable than mine at home. Esther and I could barely reach to hold hands during the movie. Sweet! Well, except for the not-holding-hands part, of course.

Three hours later, after a myriad of commercials, previews and the main attraction, I saw "Harry Potter and the Half-Blood formerly known as Prince". I haven't been this lost since I saw ... well ... *Lost*. The bit after the credits was cool though - Samuel L. Jackson as Nick Fury invites Harry to join the Avengers. I tease — the movie was pretty good, but it took Esther explaining most of the back-story to me on the way home to understand it. It's getting to the point in the series that non-fans of the books should probably just stay home. Alan Rickman's revelation that he is the half-blood prince almost seemed tacked on at the last minute, "Oh, shoot! We'd best explain the mystery of the title of the movie. At the time the best analogy I can come up with is if Lucas called the first Star Wars movie "Attack of the Sandpeople" —yes, but it was so dwarfed by the incidents of the rest of the movie as to be incidental.

Later I thought of a better analogy – what if the book was called "Harry Potter and the Potions Class".

And yes I gave away the secret of the movie – it was from 2009 for god's sake, chill out! Rosebud is a sled; Darth Vader is Luke's father; the chick on "Crying Game" was a man and Norman Bates' mother is dead.

So there.

Esther checked her phone all through the movie, dinner that night and throughout the evening. No emails, no messages. No baby. Not today.

Six

AN ENDLESS SEA OF BLAH

*I*t was Friday, September 25th. Nine years ago that day we were on our honeymoon. We were in a motel in Framingham, Massachusetts.

We were deeply in love and staying on the outskirts of a major northeastern city where we saw the ocean and visited the home and the burial site of a US President (John Adams – both Adamses for that matter).

And now, nine years later – we were deeply in love and staying on the outskirts of a major northeastern city where we saw the ocean and visited the home and the burial site of a US President.

Friday was the day Valerie had her weekly appointment with her baby doctor. We hoped the doctor would tell her enough was enough and take her to the hospital to induce. It was a slim hope but after a week of waiting we clung to any hope we could get. It was both Mark ("Luke Skywalker") Hamill's and Christopher ("Superman") Reeve's birthdays – a good omen for us nerdly types.

On our way to lunch we drove past an "Everything's 99 Cents" store. It was closed and the building and lot were for sale. I wanted to call and make an offer of ninety-nine cents for it. I could go as high as a buck forty, just to be competitive. Esther convinced me not to do it.

Late that afternoon Esther's cell phone rang. Our eyes brightened with anticipation. Esther looked at the screen ID of the caller and smiled. "It's Valerie," she said.

This is it! Finally! I can hear the conversation, "the baby is hanging onto the umbilical for dear life," she would say, "but the doctor said it is time to come out."

"Hi, Valerie," Esther said, "how are you? Uh-huh, uh-huh, that's good…"

I started to shudder. "Exposition! Provide exposition!"

After a short conversation, Esther hung up. "Valerie's doctor said they will induce on October 1st, unless the baby comes earlier than that."

October 1st. Six days away. That means unless she gives birth before October 1st, we will have been here for two weeks - the total time I planned to be gone from work. In the meantime, the clock is ticking on our motel and car rental bill. We had to extend them both another week - fortunately they allowed it. I said a few days back we were sold a bill of goods in coming to Long Island so early. Today, Esther agreed.

I was lashing out. Most people do when they have no control over a situation. It's natural; it's human. I can't blame Esther, I can't blame myself. So I blamed the adoption agency. No! It's a facilitator after all! That damned facilitator!

I was aggravated. For the last few months - and especially at this point - the adoption was out of our hands and beyond our control. It was not a situation where even our advice or opinions mattered. Or our feelings.

I felt impotent; which is ironic since impotence was what led us down the road to adoption to begin with.

"Let's go home," I said. There was no sense sticking around for six more days and then another week or so for the court paperwork to go through.

I checked the airlines. "We may as well stay put," I said to Esther.

The cost of the motel and the rental was cheaper than a flight back to St. Louis, then back to Long Island. Add to that the burden to our friends or family who would have to deliver our car to the train station in Belleville twice. Besides, neither of us would get much work done during the week waiting on news from Valerie. And what if she went into labor tomorrow?

"Oh Lord, please have someone slip castor oil in the birthmother's drink and Tabasco in her marinara sauce; break down the escalators at the mall; may she have a blow-out on the turnpike and, her AAA membership only just expiring yesterday, have her change the tire herself. You'd do it to me, who do you think you're kidding!? If you will not induce medicinally, please induce by stress. Amen."

⌒⟶

Depression hit us on Saturday. Esther caught a slight flu.

We both mentioned how much we missed our other babies on our Facebook posts. Esther brought four cats with her when we married. By 2009 they were "our" cats and two of them took an especial liking to me.

Nebula was the alpha – a beautiful Maine Coon. She was smaller than is usual for the breed and was one of the most loving cats I've ever known. Growing up, all pets belonged to my sisters. I never really had a pet of my own. Nebs was my first.

She would jump on my lap and knead my stomach before snuggling on my chest and brush my chin with her paw. Nebula was very intelligent and very sensitive to our feelings. When her first husband left her, Esther sat in a chair and cried. Nebula carried one of her kittens to Esther for her to hold.

Oliver Stone's great movie "Nixon" ends with a haunting version of "Shenandoah". I watched the movie on VHS shortly after my mother died and wept during the ending credits as that song played. The song and its arrangement got to me. Nebula sat on my lap and placed her paw on my arm to comfort me.

In April of 2009 Nebula, by now 18 years old, caught an infection and lost a lot of fur and went blind. We caught it in time and with medication she got better. We had to give her medicine twice per day and by the time we left for Long Island she got her weight and fur back and even some of her eyesight, although she still did not see very well. Now we depended on our house sitter to give her the medication. Clyde was the sitter – Valerie chose us based on the photo from his and his wife's Renaissance-themed vow-renewal. Nebula was in good hands, but I still missed her terribly.

Warlock was older than Nebs and was a beautiful white and grey male. He was the friendliest of Esther's cats and the first to befriend me. He loved having his belly rubbed and I spent hours on quiet nights doing just that. He rarely meowed or made any noise other than a purr you could hear at the other end of the house. He was as big and heavy as a cinder block – all muscle, no fat – but the gentlest animal I've known. He was my little guy and my bestest friend.

Fizzy was very shy. He was a Maine Coon and Nebula's litter mate. Fizzy was a smoky grey and afraid of his own shadow. You could barely hear his meow – it was more of a cross between a chirp and a sigh. He was beautiful. During a wedding we showed his picture to a couple who bred and raised cats professionally (they asked to see pics, being their profession – we did not foist the photos upon them). They asked if Fizzy was fixed – if not, they would like to breed him. He was. I don't know if shy Fizzy would know what to do with a female...

Mau was a mottled Egyptian Mau. She was the smallest of the four and the loudest. When it was feeding time she was so loud I would not have been surprised if the neighbors called the ASPCA. "Meow! Meow! Meow!" It was part of the background noise of our lives. Esther would shout, "Mau, shut up!" Mau would obey – but would still open and close her mouth, meowing silently.

Mau could eat four times her weight and never gain an ounce - just like most skinny humans can do. She would try to sneak food from our plates and meowed pathetically (and fruitlessly) between our legs at the dinner table. On Thanksgiving 2008 our in-laws fed Mau pieces of Turkey. By meal's end, she'd sniff at a piece of meat or skin and walk away. "Mau is full," we said in wonder, "Mau is full!"

We missed them. We missed them so much. I worried about Nebula's health and hoped they were all okay. Clyde assured us they were fine. When I told Esther that Fizzy climbed onto Clyde's lap she cried. That's how much they missed us. Fizzy didn't even climb on my lap. Mau did it only once – and we were lucky Esther had a camera at hand to prove it.

⟜⟶

*A*t dinner that Saturday night Esther said we had been there so long I picked up a New York accent. I looked lovingly in her eyes and said, "Fuck you!! ... Oh, hey, you're right!!"

⟜⟶

*H*ow can I get the birthmother into a crowded elevator that will inevitably break down mid-floor? Unless television has lied to me, that is the best way to induce labor.

⌒

*W*e spent Sunday the 27ᵗʰ driving about to the east and north to see what was over the horizon. Then back "home" to stock up on groceries for the week. We found a larger grocery store nearby and Esther was more enthusiastic about her selections this time. We found some microwavable brownies and enjoyed them that evening while watching the only thing on TV worth a damn.

I love the work of Ken Burns. He did many documentaries before *The Civil War*, but like most people that was the first time I was aware of him and his work. I saw his documentaries before *The Civil War*; I just didn't know they were by Ken Burns.

And what a great documentary that was, and still is. Like *Lewis & Clark: the Journey of the Corps of Discovery*, it was so enthralling that at times I'd forget how it was going to turn out. "Will Lewis & Clark make it home?" "Who'll win - north or south?"

For me his best doc was *Empire of the Air* - the invention of radio. I was a DJ for a decade in the 1980s and watching a documentary about my livelihood was of personal interest; plus it was a wonderfully-done film.

I loved *Baseball*, too. I join in the chorus of critics who say he spent too much time on New York and Boston. I understand the argument that baseball in the 1920s through the 1940s WAS New York, but ... Stan Musial's literal fifteen-minutes-of-fame? Really? His segment seemed tacked on like the afterthought it probably was.

Prohibition and *The Dust Bowl* were later works that had me giddy with anticipation. They didn't disappoint either. I was riveted.

I even enjoyed his stinkers like *Thomas Jefferson*.

Jazz was also a good documentary. Like *The Civil War* and *Baseball* it was one of those mega-long multi-part documentaries. My father used to say about *Civil War*: "I start watching it at any point, but then I have to watch the whole thing." I was the same way. The shorter ones I could watch in an evening, but if I wanted to watch *Baseball* Inning Three, I inevitably put in Inning Four next, then Five. The next thing I knew dawn was breaking.

Jazz wasn't that way for some reason. It made a nice change. I can watch one part, then watch the next part a few weeks later. Or skip a chapter. That's not a bad thing and I don't mean that as a critique of the show; but the fact that I'm not glued to watching the rest of it in one sitting is interesting.

That's why I do not have *The Civil War* on DVD – with all the extra footage the series now takes longer than the actual war.

We had dinner at the deli near our motel. It was a great place that served sandwiches and pizza all day – even in the morning. They did a good breakfast, too, also served all day. I am allergic to eggs so their scrambled egg pizza was out. We were never there for breakfast – by the time we dragged ourselves out of the motel room it was lunchtime. And on the few days we were out early enough to eat breakfast we were headed elsewhere.

By now I routinely read the newspaper at the deli to see what was happening locally; maybe something fun we could attend – a local concert or play. That night the PBS station debuted Ken Burns' latest documentary, *The National Parks: America's Best Idea*. It was going to air in three parts for the next three nights. It was not a two-hour affair ala *Empire of the Air* nor an epic like *Civil War.*

Ken Burns had finally come up with a subject I couldn't give a damn about. But such was the genius of Ken Burns and his production crew that I loved it! It enthralled me just like the best of his work did. Esther loved it too. It featured people from history I had never heard of (except for Theodore Roosevelt) and about events I never knew happened. I learned new things watching it!

Thank you, Mr. Burns. What a joy it is to learn new things.

Thank you again, Mr. Burns, for giving Esther and I something to look forward to during a bleak week.

Other than those six hours spread over three nights, television viewing was a drag.

The cable in the motel was abysmal. We had all the networks, WTBS, news and sports and that's about it. No Discover, History or other channel that might show anything vaguely interesting to us (although even those now seem inundated by reality shows...)

We did not have access to either of our favorite channels. I especially missed the ones that show older TV programs. TV Land and RTV with *All in the Family, Mary Tyler Moore, Emergency, Golden Girls* (am I the only heterosexual male in the world that adores that show?), *Cheers* – TV's version of comfort food. I've long given up looking for my sillier favorites – *The Bob Newhart Show, Newhart* or *Night Court*. Any of those can get me giggling like a toddler.

It must be illegal to air *F-Troop* nowadays...

And if not for the DVD sets I'd never be able to catch my all-time favorites – *Barney Miller* and (genuflecting) *WKRP in Cincinnati*; each a multi-part documentary about the real-life dealings of a police station and a radio station respectively.

The last current shows we loved were *West Wing* and *Frazier*, but neither of them are on the air except on cable channel reruns.

We liked *House* for the first few seasons. That was still on the air, why not watch it again? We liked it for Hugh Laurie. Esther and I loved his comedic skills on *Black Adder, Jeeves & Wooster* and *A Bit of Frye and Laurie*. *House* was a serious role. He deserved all the accolades he got from the show. He was Emmy-nominated three times for Best Actor and never won. The show was Emmy-nominated four times for Best Program and never won. This is more a poor reflection on the Emmys than it was on *House*. A few individual shows won for writing and so forth, though...

The trouble is by 2009 we were bored with it. A person came down with a baffling disease. Dr. House thought he knew what it was and tried to cure him or her. It didn't work and made things worse. His assistants and other doctors came up with other ideas. Some Dr. House liked; some he didn't. All the while the patient was getting worse and worse. Someone suggested it was auto-immune (my favorite drinking game next to "Hi Bob"). Then near the end someone would make a remark and House would give a smartass reply and in turn come up with the solution.

Other character: "We're sitting at the kiddie table during Thanksgiving!"

House: "Eating peanut butter instead of turkey. Turkey. Greece. Rome. Egypt. Her passport ... how many times did she go the Mediterranean?"

Other character: "Nearly every year since college. Her aunt and uncle live in …"

House: "Who cares? She has schistosomiasis!"

The next show was pretty much the same. So was the show after that. The show after that was set on an airplane, but still the same. "Ah," said the networks, "but one week it was a young girl, the next a pre-teen chess champion as smart-assy as House. Then it was a famous hip-hop star playing a pro athlete!" Oh, yes, that certainly stirs things up.

The Ken Burns documentary was over and there was nothing else to watch on the tube, so we saw *House* for the first time in years.

This time a person came down with a baffling disease. House thought he knew what it was and tried to cure him or her. It didn't work and made things worse. His assistants and other doctors came up with other ideas. Some Dr. House liked; some he didn't. All the while the patient was getting worse and worse. Someone suggested it was auto-immune (drink!). Then near the end someone made a remark and House gave a smartass reply and came up with the solution. I went to bed.

⌒

I hate motel pillows. I might as well sleep on the towels – they're thicker. But not by much…

I didn't bring my normal pillow this trip. It is a massive thing my mother made a decade before. It's the size of a normal pillow but stuffed with heavy feathers. It's like sleeping on a rock. It is about as heavy as one, too. I avoid taking it when we fly to save luggage space. I ended up rolling two or three pillows together hoping it would be hard enough to sleep on. Some nights I hit the sweet spot – but as soon as I rolled over or got out of bed to pee the pillows snapped back to their flat, thin shape making it hard for me to sleep.

⌒

The microwave brownies and part one of the Ken Burns' documentary helped keep our spirits up, but it was a long and sad weekend. By Monday the 28th, the baby was only three days away and that made us feel better. Esther found a spot she wanted to visit, so we spent most of the day on the north shore.

Esther found Sands Point Preserve on the internet. It had a castle. Esther loves castles. I was happy to go somewhere Esther wanted to go. I was also happy that Esther took a role in deciding things to do and see. In the past week I dominated that without meaning to. It showed she was calming down; the situation jelling in her mind. It was the same with the Harry Potter movie five days ago. It was only five days ago … ?

The only other time she set her foot firmly down was during a choice of where to eat. Unless there was someplace specific to go – we normally drove around until we found something interesting. I saw a middle-eastern restaurant in a strip mall right on the highway. "Let's go eat there," I said.

"It has police tape in front of it."

"No, that's construction tape – they're working on the sidewalk."

No, it was police tape after all. We didn't stop.

Esther picked The Library Café in Farmingdale simply based on the name. We weren't disappointed. It had shelves from the floor to the ceiling lined with books; and served excellent food. We were there for Sunday brunch – very crowded – and later in the week when it wasn't so busy. We took plenty of photos and loved our time there.

On Monday we went to Sands Point Preserve. It was farther west than we had yet gone on Long Island and on its north shore. It was part of the Gold Coast. The castle/mansion is called Hempstead House; owned by the Guggenheims until the estate was used as a training center by the Navy. Now it and its two hundred and sixteen acres of nature trails are open to the public.

We arrived mid-morning and had the place to ourselves. Another family pulled into the parking lot some minutes after we got there, but they quickly hit the trails and were out of sight.

Hempstead House was beautiful. We took photos of all the buildings on the grounds. Perhaps it was too late in the season or maybe it is closed on Mondays but we were unable to tour the house itself.

Gould Castle was closer to the entry of the Preserve and another beautiful and big building. It was closed too, but as with Hempstead we enjoyed walking around the grounds and taking many photos.

We took a trail to the Long Island Sound. Being a preserve, it was less kept up than Jones' Beach but this place isn't meant for swimming and lazing on the beach. We watched the sea birds and were careful not to tread on the horseshoe crabs littering the beach. I wrote "I (heart) Esther" in the sand near the surf – kind of a tradition when we are on a beach. In the distance to the east we saw the other family far ahead of us leaving the beach and going back on the trail.

Although the weather was hazy, I could see Connecticut to the north, the New York skyline to the west and Oyster Bay to the east. I wonder if I could see Sagamore Hill if it was clearer?

Esther and I slowly walked the trails around a pond and through the woods with its leaves still green in this late summer. On the way back to the main entrance/parking lot we saw a few bicyclists and more hikers. The parking lot had several dozen cars by the time we got back, but by then we were done and ready to go back to the motel. We had the entire Preserve to ourselves, took lots of photographs and enjoyed each other's company.

We decided not to go to Falaise, another house in the Preserve available for touring. I think Esther would have loved it but by now we were tired from our walk and wanted to get something to eat and go home.

For the first time in 25 years a gas station attendant pumped gas into my car. Happy 1984 everyone! Mondale-Ferraro! "Get your money for nothin', chicks for free..."

At the motel we watched part two of Ken Burns' doc on the National Parks. It was just as interesting as part one; we loved this show!

No emails, no phone calls, no baby. And the evening and the morning were the 10th day...

*T*he beautiful, warm late-summer weather ended that night. It rained heavily overnight with wind gusts at 30 miles per hour. It was wonderful to watch the storm even with our view of the corporate parking lot. I love watching storms when I know I am safe and dry inside. Watching one while inside a car is a whole different story.

Some nights earlier a helicopter landed in the lot and woke Esther (I was awake and on the computer). It was gone by morning. What strange neo-governmental intrigues went on that night, I wondered…

Esther wore a sweater or a cape (she loves capes) the rest of our time there. I was stuck with short pants and short-sleeved shirts. It was still in the eighties when we left Illinois. Fortunately I don't mind cool weather. Wearing shorts got me some strange looks, however. Well, at least I was comfortable.

I was conscious of what I was wearing twice – both times at upscale restaurants. One was during a late lunch at a place along the main highway we spotted. There were not many other customers there, which wasn't so bad. The other restaurant was at the corner of two main streets near our grocery store. Both meals were excellent and the staffs were pleasant and hard-working. But walking to our tables in shorts and tennis shoes made me self-conscious. It was very busy when we left and we went around the back and saw their outdoor dining area filled with customers. If it wasn't late September I may have seen more people wearing shorts. But everyone else was in suits – straight from work I suppose.

⌒

*A*s Esther posted on Facebook, we "finally had something on this strange adventure go smoothly." I was worried about our Amtrak tickets expiring, but the friendly Customer Service rep on the phone that Tuesday morning said our tickets were good for several months – I have forgotten exactly how long. As long as there were availabilities on the train, we could use our tickets anytime. All we had to do was call and reserve them. We booked another week for the motel and drove back to MacArthur Airport to renew the lease on the car and to add the baby seat. There was a daily fee on the seat, so I am glad we waited to get it until closer to the birth date.

In our travels we drove past a mobile home park in Farmingdale. That made me less homesick ... I was so pining for home I even missed the local trailer trash. (remember "joking on the square"?)

We ate lunch at an old-fashioned-looking diner/ice cream shop. Actual conversation overheard there - Customer: "You're the first human contact I've had today." Waitress: "Have your other contacts this morning been inhuman?" I want to go home, but I DO love this place.

The people of Long Island helped boost our morale. Everyone we met – I mean everyone – from the motel clerks to waiters and waitresses were friendly, courteous and funny.

We ate at a western-themed steakhouse on our way home from Sands Point Preserve the day before. There were horseshoes and saddles attached to the walls and country music blaring from the PA. The waiter was dressed in a plaid shirt and wore a cowboy hat. I laughed out loud when he said "Hahya doon," in that unmistakable Long Island accent. I spoke with the hostess about the restaurant while Esther was in the rest room. It was a local chain of about eight restaurants. They just opened their first one in New Jersey. Of course I have forgotten its name...

We went into a Walgreens to buy a razor and shaving cream. "Do you want a bag for this," the counter-lady said.

"No, that's okay, unless it'll make me beep when I leave." I pointed my thumb at the exit.

"Here's what I'll do for you," she said. She ripped the receipt from the cash register and wrapped it around the can of shaving cream. "There, now it won't beep when you leave."

I laughed and thanked her. At home that would have been considered a smart-ass thing to do. Not for me. Not here. I loved it and laughed about it with Esther the rest of the day.

There were children everywhere – at the diner and the day before at the western steakhouse. "Why aren't these kids in school?" I asked Esther.

It was Yom Kippur. We found out that night with a Google search. Ah ... do kids get off school for Yom Kippur? I suppose they do. They weren't going today that's for sure.

I should have known this, as southern Illinois is known for its religious diversity. We have Southern Baptists, Free Will Baptists, Missionary Baptists, General Baptists…

⌒

The 30th. The last day of September. Our last day as a couple. We will be three starting tomorrow.

Right?

Our morale was better than it had since that first week in Long Island. Since the baby was due tomorrow, this was our last chance to see some last sights.

We spotted the signs for Walt Whitman's birthplace on our Sunday drive. It was closed that day and Monday and Tuesday, so we went back on Wednesday. It had a small museum but it was packed with information about a person of which I knew very little. I read "Leaves of Grass" in high school. That was it.

His father built the home over 200 years before (between 1810 and 1814) and Esther and I enjoyed walking through it. It was just she, me and our tour guide. He was a very nice gentleman who could not be budged from his rehearsed lectures. He ignored some of my questions until we got to that part of his lecture.

We had fun befuddling him, though. You could tell he was used to school children or adults who were not raised as lower-class mid-westerns.

He picked up a piece of wood. "Can anyone guess what this is?" "A bootjack" said Esther.

"Umm, that's right… This?" He held up a large metal cylinder with a rod in the middle.

"Fireplace rotisserie."

"Ummm, yes…"

He did stump us on one thing – a toy that helped children learn to milk a cow. Some things, like this toy, were not behind the impenetrable velvet rope and we were allowed to play with it.

The interior was painted in the original colors – very soft pastels – and the furniture and household goods were of the period. The only verified belonging of Walt Whitman's parents were a knife and fork on display in the kitchen.

The Poet's Corner was lovely. Every year a children's poetry-writing competition is held. The work is judged by a famous poet (called the Poet-in-Residency) and his or her name is placed on the mosaic on the ground. I was surprised to see Alan Ginsberg's name from 1991. To be frank, I didn't recognize many of the names.

There were no poetry readings that day, but there are many events going on throughout the year – including writing and poetry workshops – and would have loved to come back. There was an event that weekend that piqued my interest. To be honest I have long forgotten what it was, but we'd be parents by then and unable to make it.

I'm glad we found it. It gave us another chance to learn something new.

$$\smile\!\!\!\!\!\rightarrow$$

Also during our Sunday drive we found Amityville. Yes, that Amityville. I was tickled. I am a horror fan from way back. I wanted to go back and find … the house.

During the week I found out what I could about "The Amityville Horror". The story generated a lot of controversy in Amityville. The city itself wants nothing to do with the publicity and sides with the debunkers. The city changed the address and the house was extensively remodeled. Horror fans still found it – the back of the house still retains the distinctive peaked roof.

Esther went with me and smiled at my joy in finding the street. We drove past it a few times until I was sure I had found the house. I went to the next street around the estuary where I spotted the dock, the boat house and peaked roof unchanged. I took photographs from the car. I didn't want to get out in case it annoyed the neighbors. If they were as kind as other Long Islanders we met, I suspect they would let me take my few pics as long as I left when I was done. I did.

Amityville is a lovely town! Lots of boutiques and places to eat. When we go back in years to come we'll spend more time there to thank them for their patience in letting a giddy horror fan snap some photographs from his car.

On the way home (and all through the trip) we enjoyed listening to what became my favorite radio station during the trip - the original WCBS. It tickled me to know that the DJ blathered in the same studio in which once performed Jack Benny and Bing Crosby. Wow. I know the odds of it being the same room, building and especially equipment are nil, but the thread is there.

⌒

*O*ctober 1st. Today Valerie will be induced and the baby born. She was scheduled to go into the hospital at 7:00 am. Except for drive-through in the nearby McDonalds we spent the day in our motel room.

We found a used book store and I bought "The Hobbit" – literary comfort food – and a few other paperbacks. Esther bought some paperbacks of her favorite genre – Regency romances. We had long since finished the books we brought or purchased in our first days here.

Why didn't we go see New York City? We were asked that a lot over the years. And the answer is the same reason why we did not leave the motel room that day.

What if the baby were born while we were away? We still weren't sure what to do when we got word the baby was born. Can we go see her? Hold her? Is there any paperwork we need to take care of?

We didn't want to be on Liberty Island and get the call. Touring New York City is an all-day investment … "the baby is born? Oh isn't that nice, we'll be back by midnight."

Next time, maybe. Not this trip.

Before we left I considered going to Hyde Park and seeing the other President Roosevelt's sights. But that would probably have to be an overnight affair. Again, we did not want to be halfway up the Hudson and have to hurry back.

I couldn't shake the thought that if we weren't available to take the baby she'd be placed in a foster home. I wanted Esther and me to be the first to hold her, to kiss her forehead, to call her by her name; maternity ward nurses aside…. They would care for her, feed her and snuggle with her too; but I wanted Abigail to hear our voices, smell us, feel our heartbeats, see our faces –

as well as newborns can see. I did not want her to be days old or weeks old before we could see her or hold her.

That's why we didn't go to Montauk or the Hamptons or Fire Island. We would have loved it and in retrospect should have gone, but we didn't want to get the call that far from the hospital.

Trips into Queens or Brooklyn were nixed for the same reasons.

Oheka Castle? Xanadu!? The building used for the mansion in "Citizen Kane" was nearby and available for viewing! I didn't learn about that until a year or so later. You BET we would have tried to go there sometime during our wait. It was a 45-minute drive from our motel. It was close to our route to Oyster Bay!

Dwelling on and moping over what-might-have-been is my favorite pastime, but for today I was concerned about one thing and one thing only – the birth of our daughter.

She will share a birthday with actors Walter Matthau, James Whitmore, Tom Bosley, George Peppard, Julie Andrews, Richard Harris, Rod Carew and St. Louis Cardinal's Mark McGwire. It is also the birthday of Randy Quaid, with whom I share a bond. At the time he made news for also running up a $10,000.00 motel bill.

"What are you mumbling about?" Esther said.

"I was just thinking, today is Thursday. How does that go? Monday's child is full of grace, Tuesday's child is in your face, Wednesday's Child had roast beef, Thursday's child had none, Destiny's Child sang 'Bootilicious'..."

"Sweetie, I think you need to take a nap…" And so I did.

With the books read and the motel view of an aircraft parking lot, there was not much else to do but troll the internet. Esther and I both enjoyed Facebook and played their games. Some of my time was also spent on World of Warcraft. In the past two weeks I leveled my characters and played many an instance and battle ground. Once late at night I was still awake and turned on the laptop to play a battleground. This was the night the helicopter landed next door.

Esther posted on Facebook – today was the day. She asked for prayers for an easy and safe delivery. "And fast," I added, "Don't forget fast or it will be a three-month delivery! Don't give God any wiggle room here!"

"Sweetie, nap."

"Yes, my dearest love. Zzzzzz..."

Esther's cell phone rang at 11:30. It was Jonathan! Here it is! This is it!

"There's been some progress, but the baby hasn't been born yet."

Facebook post at noon: Birthmother still "in labor" - this kid will be born with a driver's license.

I read through the paper and saw an ad for a Howard Jones concert that night at a local venue. I'm not a huge fan, but I enjoyed his songs on MTV – way back when they played music. His songs are very optimistic and in interviews seemed a very nice guy. I would have recognized maybe a quarter of the songs he'd perform; I am sure it was a great show. I'm also sure he will take the following Facebook post in the humor intended...

Facebook post, 1:00 pm: The baby better be born soon: the only thing left to do is a Howard Jones concert this weekend. And I'll go! GOD HELP ME, I'LL GO!!!

Facebook post, 2:00 pm: C'mon Abigail, I'm starting to take this personally. I think she's grabbed hold of an intestine and refuses to come out. {Yank, yank} "No, you can't make me!!!"

Esther's cell phone rang again at 3:00 pm. It was Jonathan! Here it is! This is it!

Facebook Post, 3:30 pm: Nothing yet! Doctor had a C-section to do (read: tough par three) and will "check in" on birth mother. She's been given pain meds. Me? None. Esther has been sedated.

Esther's Facebook Post, 4:00 pm: At 3:30 the Doctor had not been back in to check – off doing a c-section on another patient. Pains were getting stronger at that time. No word yet. Still waiting...

And that was the last we heard that day. I got McDonald's drive-through for dinner and Esther and I waited for news.

Facebook Post, 10:00 pm: good grief.

I remembered Mark Twain: "All good things arrive unto them that wait - and don't die in the meantime."

Esther's Facebook Post, 10:10 pm: No news. Will update when we know more.

By 10:30 I was ready to go to bed. I guess Abigail will be born on October 2nd. I looked up other birthdays and she will share the day with photographer Annie Leibovitz, Don McLean, Sting, George "Spanky" MacFarland, Rex Reed...

... this could be a good omen: Bud Abbott and Gandhi ...

... and Groucho Marx.

I smiled. Abigail and Groucho sharing the same birth date. It was meant to be. "I married your mother because I wanted children. Imagine my disappointment when you came along."

Okay, I can accept October 2nd.

And the evening and the morning were the 13th day...

I slept through the night; that surprised me. I expected to wake at any noise thinking it was the phone. Esther woke shortly after I did – around eight or so. We were both still lying in bed reading when her cell phone rang at ten.

It was Jonathan. Here we go again. Valerie was sent home. False alarms, maybe next week.

"Hello? Yes. Yes. Uh-huh. Uh-huh."

"Exposition! Provide expositi – ouch!! Stop throwing things at me!"

Esther hung up.

Abigail was born on October 1, 2009 at 11:10 pm, seven pounds, fourteen ounces. Twenty and three-fourths inches.

Our daughter is here!

My little baby girl is here!

...

...

...

So now what?

Seven

AND BABY MAKES ...

We leapt from our beds to tell the world – that means we typed the info on our status lines on Facebook.

Facebook was the lifeline to our family and friends for the previous two weeks. My sister said my hometown was on baby-watch with us. Dozens of people were checking our statuses for updates every day. My secretary's mother called her every morning for the past week, "Any news?"

We also called our fathers and our co-workers.

"So what happens next?" Everyone asked that. We did not know. Esther called Valerie's attorney. He didn't know the baby was born, but said he would call us later that day with details.

Then we called the adoption agency. They were back to being an agency as we were in a better mood. They did not know the baby was born either. They recommended calling Valerie's attorney to see what to do next. Damn facilitator.

We heard from the attorney mid-afternoon. He arranged for us to see the baby that night in the maternity ward. Tomorrow evening we would meet him at the hospital and he would hand the baby to us. Valerie would stay in the hospital until Saturday afternoon.

The rest of the day was a blur and seven o'clock couldn't come around fast enough. When the appointed time finally did, we took the elevator to the maternity ward just as we did that early Monday morning two decades before.

Esther says it was only twelve days before. I haven't the heart to tell her I think she is wrong...

We explained who we were to a station nurse. She phoned ... someone ... to confirm and soon led us through a door the size of a bank vault. We walked through a hallway of glass windows crisscrossed with metal mesh. Nurses wheeled babies from one room to the next.

The nurse asked us to stand by the window nearest their station and they would bring Abigail for us to watch - we could take as long as we wished. In the meantime they wheeled a baby through the hallway that was covered in thick black hair. He had more hair on his head at the tender age of one day than I did at forty-four years. Or twenty-four years. It was on his arms and legs, too. The poor baby looked like a Munchichi.

A nurse pushed a plastic baby bed into the room. Abigail laid on it with her head poking out of a white blanket with sea-green, pink and white stripes. She had a thin spread of hair on the top and sides of her head. She had acne on her cheek.

To me babies either look like Churchill or Gandhi. Abby was firmly in the Churchill camp. She had full lips – puffy lips – and thick cheeks and jowls. She had a round button nose and long eyelashes. Her ears were flat against her head. Everything looked proportioned – the ears, eyes (or at least her eyelids), mouth and nose were neither too small nor too large for her head. She looked like a baby doll.

She was so beautiful.

The baby bed had clear plastic walls on each side. A pink slip of paper was taped near the top of one wall. It read "Abigail (Valerie's last name)". Valerie agreed to call her Abigail from the start. When Abby starts to rebel as a teen and gives us the "You're not my real parents! Curry isn't my real last name" treatment, we can at least say her name was always Abigail.

Esther snuck a photo from her cell phone. I asked the nurse at the station if we could take pictures. I had brought my camera hoping we could. The nurse said, "We usually don't allow it, but you can take a few. That will be okay."

I was a good boy and only took four pictures. The first photo looked like she had snot all over her top lip, but there was a lot of grime and slime on the glass/mesh walls of the nursery as well as the plastic walls of the baby bed. What looked like copious boogers was just goo on the clear plastic wall – a strange experiment in forced perspective. The entire time she slept on her right side. She didn't move or cry while we were there.

Esther leaned in front of the window the entire time. She wore her blue cape and stood as still as stone for twenty minutes watching her daughter. I took advantage of the zoom lens to take photos around her. She smiled the entire time. Esther was as beautiful as her baby. Still is.

It was time to go. We smiled at Abigail one last time and went through the vault door, into the elevator and out into the cold dark. We went home and posted our photos on Facebook. Valerie's attorney called us - at 5:00 the next evening we could take her home – or at least to the motel room.

I thought of Valerie a lot that Friday and Saturday; and ever since for that matter. She was in the hospital from Thursday morning until Saturday afternoon. I hope Jonathan was with her most of the time. I hope her parents came to visit and brought her books and magazines to read; some paper and pen for her to write her poems.

We never got to read any of her poems. I wish we had.

We never got to see a photograph of her. I wish we had.

She was only a few corridors down. What would stop me from wandering the halls and just coincidentally passing by her room? What would stop me? Esther, Jonathan, my conscience. Meeting her face to face was strictly forbidden. It was Valerie's wish. I needed to respect that.

But I wanted to see her. I wanted to thank her. Thank you, Valerie for the nausea you suffered, for the sleepless nights you had, for allowing your body to swell and stretch, for getting winded climbing stairs and getting out of a car, for all the pain – the excruciating pain – you went through yesterday. Thank you for choosing us and validating your choice by liking us. Thank you for a beautiful little baby girl.

I thought about all the questions we had to answer and the essays we had to prepare. "Why are birth-mothers special?" I thought that one was particularly silly. I changed my mind.

She didn't want to see us. She didn't want to see the baby. I can understand that. Since she never saw Abigail, she will always be an abstraction. This is someone else's child. I never saw her, so I never made a connection with her. This is why I think her agreeing to Halloween and Christmas photos was more the ideas of the adoption agency. I don't mean that in a negative way.

This was her third child – all put up for adoption. Did she not want to see the other children – Abigail's brothers or sisters – either? Did she allow herself to see the first one and said to herself, "That was a mistake … I can't let myself see them again"?

I remember in the medieval days of the 1990s the birth-mothers weren't allowed to see or hold the baby. The child went straight from the delivery room to the arms of the adopting parents or a temporary foster home.

I mentioned that fact earlier – the thought was once the baby was in the hands of the birth-mother, the adoption was over and canceled. That's not the case anymore, and thank goodness. Let the birth-mother see that the baby is healthy. Let her see that the adopting parents are kind and loving. Wouldn't that give you a better sense of closure? "The baby will be fine. I can let her go now."

Maybe Valerie couldn't do that. Maybe she needed that abstraction, that distance.

I thought of Valerie's parents – Abigail's birth-grandparents. Did they go see the baby? Did they go see Valerie? Did they want that abstract distance, too? Were they disappointed? Were they relieved?

I thought of Jonathan – Abigail's birth-father. The nurses told us Jonathan came to see the baby through the glass partition that morning. I hope the nurses won't get in trouble for telling us about Jonathan; but it has been so long now I doubt any of them will be reprimanded. He looked through the same window at Abigail. They didn't say how long – a few minutes or an hour? We didn't ask. Maybe he wanted to be sure the baby was fine and healthy.

We met him that first Sunday night when Valerie's false alarm sent her to the hospital. I imagine the attending nurse told them we were in the waiting room that 4am. He could have told the nurse to tell us Valerie was fine and to send us home. He didn't though; he told us himself. Maybe he wanted to be sure we were fine and healthy. Esther spoke with him once on the phone. Was this his way of assessing us? "They are kind and loving; the baby is fine and healthy. I can accept them as parents for my child."

Some weeks later, at home, we set up an online digital photo sharing site. One of its features allows us to track how many people viewed each photo. We gave the password to family, our adoption agency caseworkers (they were back to being an agency by this time) and Valerie's attorney, who passed it on to Valerie.

When Abigail was about one-and-a-half we received a call from the agency – Valerie called them wanting the password. We gave it to them and there was a spike that day. Otherwise the only people looking at the photos for the past four-years-plus have been Esther and I. We promised photos until she was 18, so we're not deleting the account. Plus, it doesn't cost that much, so it's not a budget-buster.

(Actually, that telephone conversation with Esther went more like this: "Mike? I just got a call from the agency, Valerie called them ..." <THUD> "Mike? Mike? Are you there? Are you okay?" After my staff found me on the floor clutching the phone, they revived me and Esther said Valerie only called to get our password for the online photo sharing site, not that she was preg ... <THUD>...)

I hope she liked the photos.

Our last attempt to contact her was after Hurricane Sandy in 2012. We called her attorney and asked if it would be a good idea to try to phone her and make sure that she, Jonathan and their families were all right after the storm. He advised us not to. I hope they made it through without much trouble.

~ ⟋

There was not much to do that Saturday morning and afternoon except wait...

... wait ...

... with only my stray thoughts to entertain me – usually a dangerous thing.

Okay, so she doesn't share a birthday with Groucho and Gandhi – the list is still impressive: Julie Andrews, Walter Matthau and Richard Harris. Harris should please Esther-the-Harry-Potter-fan. I can teach her to sing "MacArthur Park".

Her initials (ASMC) are the same as the American Society of Military Comptrollers. My father was a comptroller at Scott Air Force Base. He was asked to join the ASMC dozens of times a year while he worked but never did.

Abigail was born October 1st. What is her sign? Is she a Sagittarian? Vegetarian? Antiquarian? I brought this up to Esther and she gave our standard response: "I wish there was some kind of universal electronic search engine we could access..." Esther clicked a few keys while trolling the Ethernet and found out — Libra!

Ironic the symbol for the daughter of an attorney is an apothecary scale.

I worried about Abigail and told Esther, "The poor baby, what if she cries? She doesn't have a mommy or daddy to hold her all afternoon and sing to her."

"The nurses will take care of her," Esther said, "she won't be alone."

We waited for 5:00 to come. During the afternoon Valerie's attorney called us. Valerie would be released later in the afternoon than expected. Valerie and her attorney (and we) wanted her home before we went into the hospital. Otherwise ... awkward ...

...really awkward.

So our meeting in the maternity ward with the attorney and Abigail was pushed to 6:00, then 6:30. We ate dinner at the Ground Round again and wasted time at a nearby used bookstore we had found. Then to the hospital where we sat in the ground floor waiting area. The gift store was about to close – it was pretty standard fare for those kind of shops. I probably bought a bottle of Coca-Cola and downed it while waiting.

The men's room was very tiny – the door into it was half the size of a regular door. I've been in larger closets. I'll bet they carved out a rest room as an after-thought.

We watched for anyone in a suit and tie, or carrying a briefcase – anything that told us this might be Valerie's attorney. A man rounded the corner a little after 6:30 and asked if we were the Currys. He wore a dress shirt and slacks and had light brown hair. He carried a satchel.

We took the elevator to the maternity ward and walked through the vault doors again. This time we sat in an examining room.

Valerie's attorney's real name should be easy to find out if you really want to dig. He is the preeminent adoption attorney of the north-east coast. I'll give him the name Ronnie.

A nurse wheeled in the dolly with the plastic-high-walled baby bed. There was Abigail again – still sleeping and just as pretty as she was the night before. The nurse asked if we had brought some clothes for her. Abigail wore the onesie Valerie had bought for her. We asked if we could keep it and Ronnie and the nurse said yes. It was the only thing we have that Valerie bought for Abigail. It's still safely hidden away.

Legally, Abigail has to be released to Ronnie and he hands us the baby outside the hospital, but we could sit in and listen to the nurse's instructions.

I was expecting something like an airline safety lecture. "When boiping yer baby, pat her back in a coicular motion like so…" I never got to hear it.

We had two nurses with us. Between Esther and I, the nurses, Ronnie and Abigail it was crowded in the small examination room. By this time I was sitting with a curtain (unintentionally) between Abby's bed and me. I couldn't see her!

One nurse said we were the first adoption of any baby from the hospital. Frankly I found that hard to believe. The hospital advertised that it is the #1 pediatric hospital in Long Island— which includes Brooklyn and Queens. First adoption? Maybe she meant the first one in which she was involved. Maybe that is exactly what she said and my head was spinning too fast to realize it.

Maybe she was right. It explains why the release was so bizarre. They did not want to give Ronnie any of the official paperwork until he explained what he needed.

One form was not signed by the doctor. Instead his signature was signed by a nurse – which is normal procedure. But Ronnie needed the birth paperwork with a "wet" signature. Ah, finally some legalese I recognized. Nurses signing doctors' names may be okay, but he needed something with the doctor's actual signature.

I deal with that in my area of the law – some forms, papers and IDs are acceptable and some are not. My clients need to show proof that they have filed their federal and state tax returns. The actual returns are acceptable, even if it is a stock form in pencil. A transcript is acceptable. The receipt proving that you filed your returns? Not acceptable. To repeat: the receipt from the government proving that you filed your taxes is not acceptable proof that you filed your taxes.

Ronnie was having the same problem. He wasn't given the forms he needed. "This is the form. We give one copy to the mother and file another with the state," the nurses said. Fine, but it's not what he needs.

Illogical? Yes. Arbitrary? Hell yes.

Ronnie dug though a stack of papers. He held up one sheet and asked the nurse, "Is this the doctor's real signature?"

"Yes," the nurse said, "but why do you need that when the other papers are fine?"

"But they are not fine for what we need, can I have this? This will do."

"Yes, but ..."

Ronnie held up the latest paper and said, "Crisis averted."

Esther and I smiled at each other. We tried to laugh (not out loud) at it all, but inside we hoped something like this wouldn't cause any delay in Abigail's release.

The nurses were friendly and professional, but let's be frank – it was Saturday night. They are probably not the ones highest on the totem pole. A day-time staff nurse would have gotten these documents signed by an attending physician in ten minutes instead of forty.

Ronnie also needed all the paperwork that would be given to a birth-parent leaving with the child. This also caused some confusion – the nurses were not sure if they were allowed to give the papers to anyone other than the birth parent – the birth-parent who had left the hospital hours ago.

The nurses, wisely-good-for-them, called their superiors to confirm what Ronnie wanted and whether to give it to him. Esther watched Abigail, still sleeping. I felt like Harpo Marx in the stateroom scene in "A Night at The Opera". Honk-honk.

Ronnie got all the paperwork he needed and asked Esther if she wanted to change the baby into the clothing we brought. He asked me to get our car and park at the main entrance of the hospital.

"But I'll miss the airline safety lecture – er – baby care lecture," I almost said. After the long scene with the nurses, I decided not to test Ronnie's patience. Honk-honk.

I kid – Ronnie was the consummate professional during the evening. He was patient and confident – without being authoritative – through the evening. He knew exactly what was needed to be done and worked well with people likely at the end of their shift that never had to do this kind of thing before. He did a great job.

I drove the car to the hospital entrance, just as I did half a decade before during Esther's battle with the fibroids. After a few minutes waiting, I walked back into the hospital. Esther, Ronnie and a nurse turned the corner and I led them to the car. On the steps Ronnie handed Abigail to Esther, who put her in the car seat.

This was the baby carrier/car seat combo we got when we rented the car. We had something like that in our car at home, too. The car seat pops off and we have instant baby carrier.

The nurse wished us luck and Ronnie said he would call us in a few days. He congratulated us and gave Esther a pat on the shoulder and shook her hand. He came around to the driver's side and shook my hand, too.

We stopped by Target to buy supplies and formula. This was during the big Asian flu pandemic and I worried about someone sneezing near our little baby. Esther said it would be all right.

We bought diapers with Big Bird on them. Ah, the crass commercialism starting from day one, well, day three. I took a Diet Coke from the mini-fridge by the check-out counter and it was warm. Every bottle was warm – the fridge wasn't working. The only other mini-fridge with Coke products was several aisles down, but I found a cold bottle of the stuff eventually. We each used the restroom then back to our motel with our little girl.

…our little girl…

I learned how to use the camera timer and took pictures of the three of us. Then some photos of Esther feeding Abigail for the first time. She took photos of me holding her and mugging for the camera. For the first time – for us anyway – Abby's eyes were open and she squeaked and cooed.

She had beautiful dark eyes – nearly black.

I tested her grasp reflexes.

Grasp reflexes were mentioned in all those books I read months before. Abigail grabbed my thumbs tightly in her little hands. This is, supposedly, a throw-back to the days when babies held on for dear life to the hair on their homo-habilis mommas as they climbed from tree to tree; this was back in the day when the appendix and the tonsils had a purpose.

My little Abigail snuggled on my chest. She was as tiny as the baby dolls we bought for her.

It was October 3rd. It was exactly – exactly (even to the hour) – nine months ago I asked Esther if she would consider adopting.

Abigail was more beautiful than she was in the hospital. Pouty lips, round nose, prominent eyebrows, deep dark eyes, feathery hair and soft skin. We've only had her for two hours and I already loved her. I loved her with all my heart.

She slept very well that first night. Esther did too. I didn't. I never do. We got into a routine quickly though – eat, sleep for an hour, change the diaper, sleep about two more hours, repeat.

Ronnie called Sunday to tell us the adoption paperwork would be next-day airmailed to Illinois on Monday. When the IL Department of Child and Family Services (DCFS) approves the paperwork and faxes the approval-stamped forms back to him, we can go home. I asked if we should apply for New York driver's licenses, he said it should be all right. The approval of the interstate compact on the New York side will be quick.

Later in the day we got a call from our attorney in Chicago – that is, the adoption attorney appointed to us by the agency. We received an introductory letter from her some weeks ago and had not heard from her since. Until now there was not much for her to do.

She hoped the interstate compact would be approved by the end of the week, but it takes several days to process the paperwork. The paperwork is necessary for the Interstate Compact for the Placement of Children (ICPC).

ICPC is the law in all fifty 50 states, the District of Columbia, and the U.S. Virgin Islands. It controls how to adopt a child from another state other than to adult relatives. You can't just say, "we want a Rhode Islander! I like their spunk!" Rhode Island has to approve it, in their own spunky way. Then your home state has to approve it, too. So if your governor has a long-standing feud with, say, Utah, your adopting of an Utahan child might not be approved. The home studies and medical records are all examined, poked and prodded by both states.

Ronnie sends the paperwork – including the medical papers that gave the nurses such a fit – to New York's ICPC office (easy), New York has to approve the adoption (easy), then the paperwork is sent to Illinois' ICPC office (easy). Then Illinois approves the paperwork (ah, here's where it gets thorny…), notifies Ronnie (easy) and we go home (oh god, let it be easy).

If we don't follow this procedure, or we leave New York prior to being approved, well…

Knock knock, "Hi, were from the government. You left New York before you were supposed to and the adoption is void. Where is the little one?"

So we are back to waiting. Only instead of waiting for the baby to be born, we wait for two of the largest and bureaucratically-ensnarled states of the Union to approve a piece of paper.

So, where is the nearest Department of Motor Vehicles?

And in the meantime we had a baby to take care of…

She has the hiccups. How can I scare her to get rid of them? Tell her about the ICPC procedure? Tell her how much college will cost when she is 18?

The outer eyelids pointed up. She looked Near-Asian.

And she was a deep yellow. Jaundice is common in newborns and the nurses told us to give her indirect sunlight. Normally this would be easy; but since we have a south-facing motel room, the sun burns through the windows all day as if we were a probe orbiting Mercury. We managed.

What we couldn't manage — at least at first — was Abigail's severe stomach cramps. She didn't vomit, but you could tell the formula was making her tummy hurt. You could see the muscles cramp. The baby cried and cried. We couldn't get her to stop.

Esther cried. She was scared. "What do we do?" She remembered a co-worker back home was a retired nurse. Esther got herself under control and called her.

"What were we feeding her," Esther's co-worker asked.

"Enfamil."

"Try switching to Similac." Weeks later Abby was diagnosed with reflux. We had to thicken her formula with rice and keep her head elevated while she slept by putting a small pillow under one side of the mattress to make it tilt a little.

So it was back to Target to buy some Similac to see if that worked. In the meantime, Abby's tummy still hurt. Well, with reflux it is not the tummy but the esophagus getting burned by stomach acids that cause the pain.

It was bedtime by now and we weren't sure what to do.

"I can sit in the chair and hold her while she sleeps upright," I said. We bought a small baby bed for her — basically a fancy low-walled box that set on the bed. Esther slept beside her and the thick plastic walls prevented her from rolling over the baby. Tonight I would stay up and hold her. Tomorrow the Similac would hit and we would see if that helped with the painful gas.

From ten in the evening until about four I sat on the chair by the window. I patted my daughter softly on the back. I crossed my legs; I put both legs up on my bed, then one, then the other. Abby slept. It was a stationary chair and the back of it only reached to my mid-shoulders. If I wanted to lay my head down, I would have to scrunch down until my head reached the chair's back. This would have Abby laying flat on my chest and would reactivate the reflux. So I sat with my head up for six hours. I may have nodded off for a few minutes – I remember my head dropping down to my chest. It startled me! I didn't want to fall asleep and drop her. That was not likely, though. Possible, but not likely.

If it were a lounge chair I could prop my feet up, lay back and keep her head elevated and snooze a little myself. But … My neck and legs were quite stiff when Esther relieved me at 4:00am. I went to bed and woke up around ten. The baby had been awake a few times and was lying in her portable side sleeper on Esther's bed. Abigail was lying flat! The Similac worked!

⟿

On Monday we decided it was time for a change. We might be leaving for home in a matter of days but we wanted to leave this motel. It was a wonderful place to stay, but the last two-and-a-half weeks were tense. We were tired of our view of the airplane graveyard. Plus, if I was going to stay up nights holding Abigail, I wanted a better chair with a higher back or a lounger.

We made reservations for a week at the Hilton Garden Inn in Islip. It cost as much as our Extended Stay but without a kitchenette.

We took one last trip to the Target for supplies. And we ordered take-out from the deli we had come to love a few blocks away. We called for pick-up and within a few seconds the deli called us back. They did not recognize the cell phone's area code or exchange and wanted to make sure we weren't a crank call.

We drove to the deli and when I asked for our order the waitress explained why they called us back. I said I understood – she probably doesn't get many calls from Illinois. She asked why we were visiting and I explained why we were in Long Island. I told the waitress/deli clerk how much we loved the place and how we'd miss it. She was a beautiful young lady in her mid-20s. She had long black hair tied in a high pony tail. She had dark eyes and a pale, gaunt face.

"Oh my gawd," she said in that unmistakable accent. "I want to have a baby so bad! You have a brand new baby?"

"Yes, she's in the car with my wife, would you like to see her?"

"Oh, yeah!" She turned and yelled at another counter clerk. "I'll be outside; I wanna go see their baby!"

She followed me to our car parked in front of the deli. Esther gave me an odd look as we walked to the car. She was in the back seat with Abigail.

I opened up the back door closest to the baby. "She wants to see our new addition," I said to Esther.

"Oh my gawd," the waitress said, "she is so beautiful!"

"Thank you," said Esther with a big grin.

"I want a baby so bad! She's beautiful."

"We think so, too," said Esther, ignoring the first sentence.

The waitress and I went back inside where she told any co-worker who would listen about her desire to have a baby and how pretty ours was.

The food was ready and I paid and gave her a big tip. "Congratulations on your beautiful little baby," she said as I waved goodbye.

I want to go home, but I do love it here.

We stepped out of the elevator of our motel into the lobby.

"Is that your grandbaby?" The clerk asked. I will be asked this twice more – by a waitress at a Pasta House and the other in the drive-through in McDonalds. When I explained she was my daughter it embarrassed the hell out of them and they apologized. I told them both it was okay and the mistake was understandable.

We told the motel clerk she was our baby and we were adopting her.

She was quick to defend herself. "Well, you weren't pregnant all this time and now you have a baby."

"It would be kind of confusing," Esther said. We had been waiting all these weeks for her to be born. Now she is ours, we explained. She said how pretty Abigail was and we thanked her.

We didn't get to know the clerks by name, but we recognized them enough to say "good morning" or "good evening". They said goodbye to us when we left. We told them what a wonderful motel it was. It will always be in our memories. Good memories…

⌒⟶

The new motel room was a little larger than the old one, the bathroom was the same size, and the chairs were bigger. It did not have a kitchenette, only a small refrigerator and a microwave; as well as daily concierge and room service. If we didn't want to cook in, eat out or get carry-out, we could have six mozzarella sticks for $12.00 sent right to our room. We wouldn't be doing that often, but it's nice to know we could if we need to stay in with the baby.

And we had another south-facing room. So much for indirect sunlight.

It had a huge lounge in the main floor. Now I have a place to sit with the baby while Esther slept and not worry about making a lot of noise … and vice-versa.

Better cable! Dozens of stations! Esther can watch her political talking heads; I can watch *The Golden Girls*. The comedy duo of Bea Arthur and Estelle Getty is up there with Abbott & Costello.

The motel had a shuttle to the airport: this fits into our plans for returning the rental car when we got the word we could leave.

The move did us good and improved our morale. Abigail was feeling better after the switch to Similac. The ICPC paperwork was in the process of being approved. We were nearly home.

⌒⟶

Sometime on that Tuesday October 6th after we moved into our new room, Esther set her cell phone on her laptop. She thought nothing of it until she tried to turn on her computer.

Nothing.

I mean nothing. It was fried.

Esther did not realize she set her phone next to the touch pad and below the keyboard. You forget such details when you are three weeks away from home and taking care of a newborn. For the duration, we were down to my laptop for internet. The games we played on Facebook and my World of Warcraft kept us sane during this long stay. Also, it was nice booking and rebooking our rental car, motels and trains and looking for stores and tourist sites.

But now we had the baby to keep us occupied and better cable between shifts; having only one computer wasn't as bad as it would have been the week before.

⁓

*R*onnie called us with more news. Ronnie, Valerie and Jonathan went to court that morning to officially terminate their parental rights. Ronnie said it went "textbook". Jonathan admitted paternity, Valerie said she was terminating her rights of her own free will and was not coerced or paid or promised anything by doing so. We were not to attend – we didn't know about it until it was finished. I wouldn't want to go anyway.

Abigail now belongs to the sovereign state of New York, not us. Not yet. Now that Jonathan and Valerie have surrendered their rights, all the legal paperwork showing that surrender plus the hospital discharge papers and the medical records that Ronnie and the nurses' fought over will be submitted to New York. The ICPC can begin.

Wait, wasn't that supposed to have been done Monday?

Well, that's okay. It has begun. Perhaps tomorrow, maybe Thursday, all the "I"s will be dotted and the "T"s crossed and we can all go home.

Right?

I celebrated the good news the only way I could, considering the situation…

I shaved.

I have never been able to grow a beard or a mustache. I tried once in college and got about two weeks into it when the itchiness drove me to the bathroom with razor and shaving cream in hand.

I've not shaved since we left home. Nineteen days later the itching passed and I was left with soft, yellow, downy-like hair on my cheeks and neck. The hairs on my chinny-chin-chin were bristly. The vague mustache was starting to fluff and curl.

But it was in no way a healthy-looking set of facial hair. Since we will be going home in the next few days (right?), and thus back to work; the facial fungus had to go. Too bad. I'll miss strangers giving me bibles and canned food as I passed them on the street. "Oh you poor man," one lady told me and gave me a dollar bill.

Another milestone on this happy day: for the first time I changed Abigail's diaper.

"Pig!" I hear some of you shout. "You made your wife do all the work over the past three days?!" To which I reply, "Fuck you!"

Sorry about that. After nineteen tense days away from home and work, the cracks are showing. We have the baby to take care of and that is a 24-hour job.

Before the baby we were desperate for something to do. We'd visit famous sights, go see a movie, go shopping; but in between times ... what?

Esther had schoolwork to do. That helped. She could post on message boards, upload her homework and participate in online lectures.

Me? I can't play World of Warcraft and Farkle 24/7. So I waited for something to pop up on Yahoo Messenger.

I had a few instant messages since I left the office: what do you think we should say to the client about this new development? What kind of motion should we file with the court? But only four or five of those. It was mainly things like "how are you doing?" "Any news?"

It was wonderful of them to ask and I will always appreciate my staff, the other associate and my boss for their care and concern. And their patience.

I am amazed how much my office has changed in the years since. If this were happening now - were I "stuck" somewhere with no chance of getting back anytime soon – I could see clients through a Yahoo video call. Some potential clients would have thought that impersonal, but I think most of them would not have cared; especially if we explained why we need to do this over the computer.

Clients, especially my clients – people in financial straits wanting to know their options in filing bankruptcy – feel more comfortable with a hands-on, local person and local staff. If they're treated like they are on a conveyor belt – they will not hire you.

Some potential clients would not care – as long as the person on the phone spoke understandable English. These same folks also wouldn't mind going online and talking to a generic petition preparer. They prefer the distance.

Mostly, though, they want someone here they can talk to, to say hello to when they drop information off. They like a staff that will tell them "good morning". They want to know someone will give a damn about them.

I don't think a video consult would be too bad. If it would drive away a potential client odds are something else would have driven them off, too. People under financial stress know what it's like to be trapped – with collection agencies tormenting them and lawsuits sucking out fifteen percent or more of their income and not knowing if they can dig themselves out.

They come to me as a last resort, I suppose. "This is the last thing I want to do." I hear that a lot. Sometimes they add, 'nothing personal of course."

Sometimes…

Sometimes they treat me as if I were just left of the devil. But not too often. Those are the kind of people that would use a video consult as an excuse not to come back.

One or two video conferences a day and documents emailed for my approval would have made me feel useful over the first fourteen days. Then, after we got the baby from the hospital, I would have asked for no more appointments so I could spend time bonding with her and taking care of her.

But the point is I changed her diaper. Not bad for a first try. She cried. I almost cried. But I didn't make a mess. Not that time, anyway. But at this early stage there wasn't a lot to worry about. It was basically removing the diaper and wiping off the processed cheese spread from her butt and girlie parts. Then try to throw away the diaper without touching it.

Fortunately the motel trash bins were near our room. About four or five times a day we dumped many a diaper into them.

In the previous motel the trash bins were in a room hidden behind the elevators. Near that utility room was one of the more expensive suites. Once I walked past the suite when the maid cleaned it and I got to peek inside. Huge beds, a kitchen table as well as a kitchenette. Sweet suite. We liked our new room in our new motel; but if we had originally gotten the big one, we might have stayed.

Especially since it faced north…

I was in a car crash in 1999. It was a Sunday and I was shopping in Carbondale and Marion. I picked up some files and other papers from the Marion branch office and headed home on Interstate-57. A summer gully-washer formed ahead of me and I slammed into it.

There was a police car behind me most of the trip. That didn't bother me – I had the cruise control set at 65 and he kept a safe distance behind me. On a typical hot and humid southern Illinois summer day, the tar and oil from the highway bubbles to the top of the road. When it rains heavily the oil and tar mix with the water to make the highway incredibly slick. If one starts to hydroplane there is no traction and braking becomes useless.

I hydroplaned.

My car slipped into the grassy median between the north and south-bound lanes. I swiped the divider and slammed into the overpass support. The impact set off the airbag – the police officer said it saved my life.

When it was over, I sat in my car in a daze. I wasn't quite sure what had happened. It was very quiet.

The impact had pushed the audio cassette tape dangling in front of the player into it. This turned off the radio and turned on the cassette player. This is why it was so quiet.

It was a home-made cassette of new age music. The throbbing lilt of synthesizers flowed from my speakers.

"Oh my. I've died and gone to heaven," I said. I saw the cassette player was running and laughed at my silliness. I ejected the cassette.

This turned on the radio. The station was in the midst of a thrash metal song.

"Oh, god, I've died and gone to hell! Falwell was right!"

By now the police officer following me parked and walked up to my window. He knocked and asked if I was all right. By now the rain stopped and the storm passed.

My car was totaled. It looked so bad when the tow truck appeared the driver asked if there were any fatalities. I had a bruise on my knee and burns on my inner forearms. The officer explained that my hands had a death grip on the steering wheel and when the airbag activated it caused a rug burn of sorts on my arms. The knee was bruised from pressing it against the door – another kind of death grip.

A few weeks later a friend named Esther also totaled her car. A semi turned right from the far left lane of a four-lane road. The driver didn't seem to care that her car was in the right lane next to him – he turned in front of her and crushed her car. She managed to duck down enough to avoid being decapitated. She hurt her neck and back and took physical therapy for a while. The truck driver is presumably still crushing and smashing cars and otherwise being a danger to others to this very day without repercussion…

Since she had no rental car clause on her insurance, and couldn't afford a rental on her own, she called her friend Mike for rides to work and our Friday night game sessions – his insurance included a rental, you see. Mike & Esther got to know one another and …

So out of the deal I got a new car thanks to my insurance keeper policy ("I wish I could get a new car for free." "You can if you want to crawl out from under a bridge to get one…") and I found the love of my life. I also got an intense and manic phobia of driving a car in the rain.

I'm fine as a passenger in heavy rain, but not as a driver. I don't even like light rain – I'll drive in it but it makes me nervous.

⟜

I drove Esther and Abigail to a Babies-R-Us in a shopping center several miles south of the airport. We ran into another big gully washer (or whatever Long Islanders call those sudden and intense storms). I tried to persevere, but soon I parked under an overpass and cried. "I don't like driving in the rain." I chanted to myself. Esther, in the back seat with the baby, patted my back and told me we would be fine.

When the rain stopped we went to the Babies-R-Us. I sat in the car to get myself under control while Esther and Abigail went in for more diapers and formula. I took some deep breaths and wiped my tears. Stop being a pussy, I told myself, go inside and help your family! And I did so.

Esther thinks part of my breakdown was because of the stress of being away from home and work. Probably.

Still, near the Babies-R-Us were a Borders book store and a two-story Burger King! Being trapped here isn't SO bad…

Despite such little delights we were both very homesick and I think the baby picked up on the tension. She cried. A lot. We thought she might already be colicky. Esther called her work-mate again and she recommended some baby gas medicine.

The change in formula and the gas medicine helped! Abigail slept better - and so did we - although her burps and toots would have shamed a teamster.

And by now we had the feeding/burping/diaper thing down. We mixed the formula and water into a condom-shaped plastic bag (well, it looked like a huge condom – I mean the kind Errol Flynn or Forrest Tucker would use) and popped the bag into the hollow bottle. You press up on the bottom of the condom to squeeze out all the air – until the formula squirts or oozes out of the top. The bottle is baby ready.

The more air you can squeeze out – the less gas Abigail will have. Got it. No worries!

$$\sim$$

Ronnie called us on Thursday, October 8th. The state of New York cleared us for interstate travel.

"Woo-hoo!" I said, "We can take the train outta here tomorrow!"

Nope. Illinois has to approve it, too. The paperwork is scheduled to arrive in Springfield tomorrow at 9:00 am.

Um, wasn't that supposed to have been done Monday?

The timing could not have been worse. If the Department of Children and Family Services – or whoever would be in charge of such things – verbally approves our taking Abigail to Illinois Friday, we can go home.

That Monday was Columbus Day. If they didn't approve it on Friday, it will be Tuesday. Or later.

One of my very best friends from law school works in Springfield for the Illinois senate. "Maybe we can call him and see if he can help," Esther said. I said I doubted that he could. We didn't call him.

Esther got on Facebook and asked friends to pray the paperwork was on the top of the anonymous bureaucrat's pile.

I was more direct: "Everyone pray that we get verbal approval tomorrow. Pray! I SAID PRAY DAMN YOU!!!! Er, rather, we appreciate your prayers at this juncture..."

I was desperate and angry. "Let's go home. Who's going to know?"

"We're not doing anything that will get us in trouble," Esther said. She was right of course. And if it came to it I would have stayed. I just felt like saying it out loud.

That evening we ate at a 1950s-style diner. The waitress oohed and aahed over Abigail. An older couple came over to see her, as did a small child (Abby does that now – she's done that ever since she's been able to walk – babies love to look at babies).

It was a wonderful meal. It was a wonderful diner filled with wonderful people.

It gave us no joy.

⟅⟆

Illinois is an hour behind New York, so the offices there would not open until 10:00 a.m. our time. We weren't expecting any news from Ronnie until noon. In the meantime I posted to anyone willing to read on Facebook about the Nobel Peace Prize awarded that day to the President. I also posted "(t)hanks for all the prayers for us getting to go home today. No luck though. Anyone want to join me for prayers to Wotan? Baal? Any deity that will listen?"

Noon passed. So did 1:00. Then 2:00. Then 3:00. Esther lay down in bed and cried. A few minutes later she fell asleep. The baby was fed and she slept as well. I stayed up and played World of Warcraft and waited for the baby to wake up.

Soon it was four o'clock our time; three o'clock in Illinois.

Three o'clock the Friday before a three-day weekend at a government office. By now people were sneaking between the partitions and cubicles, jumping through the bathroom windows and pushing their cars out of the parking lots. Once out of earshot they'll start the engine and get the hell out of there. The smart ones took that Friday off months before – those left were the bitter employees who were too late to get their vacation requests approved in time.

Ties are loosened; wine and beer bottles are opened. The radio plays. "Two more hours and we're outta here," someone shouts from across the room. Is someone smoking? That's doesn't smell like tobacco...

I took my frustrations out on my fellow WOW gamers. When I had finished at four o'clock I started a Facebook post; I took my previous post to its inevitable conclusion:

"Oh Mighty Baal, please strike dead those who decided we should not be allowed to go home this weekend and curse their spawn to the third generation."

I was ready to hit "Send" when Esther's cell phone rang. She woke up and said hello in a groggy voice.

It was Ronnie.

We were approved to take the baby home.

I told Esther to shut off the phone in case he calls back and said it was a mistake. We would crinkle some foil in front of the phone. "Sorry, bad signal – we're already in Pennsylvania – what? What?"

I could not have made the timing up. If I wrote it as part of a story the editors, critics and the reading masses would tear it to pieces. "What kind of melodramatic shit is this?"

I added to my Facebook post: "- hold on! As I type this we got our call! We're going home!!! Jesus came through at the last minute! Hurrah for Jesus (but you cut it pretty close there, Godboy! Watch it!!)!!"

Esther was a little more pleasant. She always is… "Praise God!!! We are cleared to take Abigail home. Thanks for all the good thoughts and prayers. We'll be offline a couple of days. Facebook by cell phone for now. Please ignore Mike's post."

Harrumph!

It was 4:15 local time on a Friday before a three-day weekend. What if it's too late to book a train and all the seats were full? We might be stuck here anyway!

I called Amtrak. They transferred our tickets to the next day with little trouble. I lost my temper at the poor customer service lady who didn't seem to understand that we requested a sleeper car. I feel bad about that, but she was keeping us from going home. Ah well, I won't be the last irate customer she will have.

We asked the motel's counter clerk about their shuttle to the airport and to the nearest Long Island Railroad station. Yes, we can take the shuttle in the morning, she said, we just need to make reservations. We did.

We drove to the Kinko's across the highway and mailed home as much as we could fit into shipping boxes. We returned the rental car to the airport. We thanked the clerk for being open (it was after five by now) – but I expect they are open late anyway for later flights. The hourly motel shuttle took us back for our last night in Long Island. We had room service (remember the $12.00 mozzarella sticks?) and, except for what was needed in the morning, stuffed the rest our belongings into suitcases.

We decided long ago to take the train home because airlines don't allow babies less than two weeks old to fly. Ironically, had we not been approved until after the holiday weekend, she would have been old enough to fly. Plus we didn't know how the baby would travel — a car trip could have been awful.

Hindsight shows we could have driven – Abigail was an excellent passenger. But we would have had to find some way to rent a car, van or SUV going one-way. They were available but it would have cost nearly the same as the train. Plus add motels and food during the long trip and it would have been more expensive. More convenient, but more expensive.

A mong the many nice things about babies is there is no need for an alarm clock. Among the many horrible things about babies is there is no need for an alarm clock. By the time the alarm rang at four that Saturday morning we had already fed and changed Abigail, showered and packed our last bits of belongings. I paid our bill (actually Capital One did and I paid them – still paying them for that matter) and pushed our luggage carrier to the motel shuttle.

Other people were on the shuttle for the Long Island Railroad station that morning too. That surprised me – it was 4:30 for gosh sakes! It took a long time to get to the station, and the train pulled up just as we paid for our tickets to Penn Station. We found a nice niche to ourselves and settled back for the next hour or so.

The ticket-taker walked past a few times. We laughed as men bolted the train during stops as the ticket-taker approached. They had no ticket and were riding for free. Thieves!

Soon we were at famous Penn Station. I thought about looking around, but decided against it. It was a long walk to the Amtrak station, but the way was clearly marked. There were a few homeless people sleeping in the hallways as we passed. We don't have much of that in our small town so it was hard for me to ignore them. I thought about the hundreds of people that pass by without as much as a glance. Are they cold for doing so? No, not really; but that in itself is also a problem, isn't it?

A friendly Amtrak lady checked us in and told us that since we had a sleeper car for the trip from DC to Chicago, we could stay in the VIP lounge at all three stations. We were prepared to lay on benches and wait, but instead spent our layovers on comfy couches with clean bathrooms and complementary sodas, tea, coffee and snacks.

I kept Abigail snuggled on my chest while in the lounge at Penn Station. The train to Washington DC was delayed in Boston for several hours. I wasn't worried about missing our connection – it wasn't for another twelve hours.

Esther took some photos of Abigail and me trying to snooze. The VIP lounge was the perfect tonic. We got to relax. It reminded me of going to Long Island – this was happening. Really happening. We are forty-eight hours from home.

The train to Washington DC arrived late that morning. We were herded to the train and found a row to ourselves.

Directly behind us sat a lady and her seventeen children. Esther insists to this day there were only three, but it is not humanly possible for only three kids to make that much racket. The mother had a distinct accent – she came from the land down under – so I dubbed her the Australian Octo-mom.

I sat next to the window with one of the Australian Octo-mom's litter behind me. For the last hour of the trip the boy chanted, "please please stop"; as if willing the train to arrive at the station sooner. After fifteen minutes I, too, wished the train would arrive at the station sooner.

Eventually Australian Octo-mom told the boy to be quiet. "Yes, please please stop," I said loud enough to be heard.

The Washington DC Amtrak VIP lounge was packed. Standing room only. The three of us had to stay in a conference room with its long table and many chairs. Before going into the VIP lounge we bought some pizza slices and other snacks for lunch. The attendant said no food was allowed. "Okay," I said and turned to Esther to take the baby carrier, "you stay out here and get something to eat. I'll watch the baby and then you can watch the baby while I eat."

I didn't intend to be mopey, but we must have looked pitiful enough for the attendant to say, "Well, you can go on in if you keep the food in the conference room and clean up."

"Oh thank you, nice lady..."

After a few hours the bulk of the travelers left the VIP lounge and Esther and I moved into the main area.

We spent Washington DC to Chicago in our sleeper car. It was too small for two people, especially two large people with a baby. We didn't mind - it allowed us more time to bond with Abigail in that Stockholm Syndrome sort of way. And the meals were fantastic - the best crab cakes I have ever had! If it were the two of us it would have been very romantic.

We felt claustrophobic in the small room so we kept our door open to the hallway. The fellow across from us, who spent his trip typing on his laptop, did likewise. The porter knocked anyway and asked when we wanted dinner. While we were in the dining car, he said, he would set up our beds.

I had the upper berth. I leaned on the wall of the train car as I slept and its vibrations and its chugga-chugga-clang-clang lulled me into a deep sleep. I woke at two wondering what was wrong – the train had stopped. Ah, we stopped at Pittsburgh for a long layover. The baby was awake and Esther fed her.

The baby woke again at 4:00 a.m. I decided to shower and wake for the rest of the day.

The shower was steaming hot and wonderful. It was in a large restroom so I was careful not to drench the commode next to me. It was as big as our sleeper berth.

I took Abigail to the dining car and sat with her while watching the sun rise. The crew came in and prepared breakfast. By six, a few other passengers walked in. I managed to eat a grapefruit one-handed. Esther slept in and met us in the dining car for her breakfast. They let me stay in the dining car with her. They had a strict "there's-a-lot-of-people-coming-in-here-so-eat-and-get-out" policy. No one minded my staying, though.

Two cousins from Manchester, England sat at our table. They were taking a train tour of the United States. They were a joy to talk to. Abigail's foot slipped out of her blankets and she stretched it out. It was close to the cousin on my left. "Abigail, don't stick your foot in this nice lady's face," I said in a baby sing-song.

"Ooo, oi luv baby feet," she said and kissed it. "Mwuh mwuh!" I since adopted that into a game with Abby. "Feets! I love baby feets! It's my favorite flavor of feets! Mwuh mwuh!"

The cousins loved the jellies and jams in the tiny packets. She said they don't have this kind of grape jelly at home. I said she should take one or two. "Oo, oi couldn't steeeeal et."

"No, it's okay, they don't mind if you take one or two. But not a lot. Put it in your pocketbook, it's all right," I said. She covered the circular plastic packet of grape jelly with her hand and snuck it into her purse. I imagine it still setting in a display case in her home next to her whimseys. "An American helped me steal this," she says.

As we walked back to our sleeping berth after breakfast, a lady called to us from her room. "Is that the nine-day-old baby?" Her door was open, too, but her berth was bigger than ours. "The porter told us someone had a baby on board." She came out to see Abigail.

"Yes, she's ten days old now," I said. "She's aged a day, I've aged ten years." During the trip a few others asked if this was "the nine-day-old baby." Word spreads quickly on a small train.

The Chicago VIP lounge had no problem with our bringing in food. We had a four-hour lay-over before our last trip to St. Louis. So we got some sandwiches and drinks from the kiosks at Union Station and ate an early lunch.

In our section of the lounge there was one other man looking at photographs. I shut off the TV and he said, "Excuse me, I was watching that." I reminded myself I was no longer in friendly Long Island but back in Illinois – where our governors make our license plates. I was officially a lawyer again. And a notary, for that matter.

"No, you weren't. You were thumbing through your photographs."

"You can move over there where there's no television."

"You can move over THERE where there's a television on and people are actually watching it. If you tell me what the program was, I'll turn it back on."

...

...

"I didn't think you could." I turned it back on anyway. He was gone within the hour. By then someone had turned the channel, without a protest from him, and watched a Sunday morning sports talk show.

I walked around Chicago's Union Station for a while, then it was Esther's turn. I had been here a few times before – this was where they filmed some of "The Untouchables" with Kevin Costner and Sean Connery. I stepped outside into the freezing air. This was the first time I had been out in the open since leaving Long Island. It was bone-chillingly cold that October morning. I had on a thin shirt and blue jean shorts and that Chicago wind cuts right through you even when you are dressed for it.

It was eighty degrees when I left home…

⌒

*C*hicago to St. Louis was the shortest and slowest part of the trip, or so it seemed. There was a half-hour wait outside of Joliet. It was agony.

We didn't have a sleeper so we again sat in coach in a row to ourselves.

Behind us a young lady yelled at her boyfriend Chris for not wanting to pick her up. "You'd pick up your sister who you hate, but not me?!"

During one of the lady's tirades Esther's cell phone rang. It was her father. I couldn't resist saying out loud when it rang, "Oh hi, Chris! Yeah, thanks for coming to pick us up!" Esther told me to be nice and be quiet.

Worst of all was Captain Dig-Me. He came in with his wife and two kids at Joliet. The kids sat far in the front of the coach car. His wife sat a few rows behind us. He plopped down in the row ahead of us across the aisle. He sat next to an elderly man with one of those World War II caps that stated his regiment.

He talked.

And talked and talked.

He asked the veteran a question, then go on about himself and how he related to that answer. After an hour or so I noticed the talking had stopped. I looked up. Captain Dig-Me was still there but the veteran had gone. Did he jump out the window? There was no broken glass and I would have heard him jump. He probably went to sit in the snack bar for some deserved peace and quiet. He fought Hitler and Tojo for this?

The crowded train thinned as we got further south. Most of the passengers got off at Bloomington and the coach car was half-full. I went to the snack car a few times – the rest of the train was also half-full. We thought about moving, but decided to stay put – it would be a hassle fighting our way back through the cars to get to our bags.

Outside of Springfield, Captain Dig-Me pulled out a mandolin from his luggage and started playing. Badly. He looked around, in the hopes someone would ask him to play something or make some comment. Any excuse for him to get attention.

No one took the bait. By now we were all onto him…

When that didn't work he stretched out his arms and legs to block the aisles. Some of us took solace in making him move. "Excuse us," we barked.

Fond and familiar cities rumbled past: Springfield, Alton…

By six that evening we pulled into the St. Louis station. My father was there to meet us.

Two days before, late that frantic Friday afternoon, we called him to give him the news. "So you'll be home Sunday night," was the first thing he said.

"How did you know that?"

"Your sister called me. She saw it on the computer." He volunteered his time working for the city clerk, and the clerk and his secretary kept a Facebook watch to give Dad all the news.

And now here is my father waiting for us at the station. I have never been happier to see his face in my adult life.

"Hi, Dad."

"Did you have a nice trip? Where's that bad mandolin music coming from?"

"I'd rather not talk about it. I'd like to introduce you to your new granddaughter."

He said he finally has a brown-haired brown-eyed girl; he has always wanted a brown-haired brown-eyed girl.

He drove our car to the train station. We had a baby seat installed for free that summer by the fire department during one of those baby-seat safety seminars they give a few times a year. When we got south of Mascoutah, Abigail cried. Esther asked us to pull over so she could feed the baby – Dad and I rode in front.

We told her to take her out of the seat and feed her.

"We're not supposed to do that."

"No jury in the world will convict us. All we need is one mother on it…" It's good to be a lawyer again.

We went to my sister's house in Coulterville. She took plenty of pictures and plenty of children looked at their new cousin. My sister held Abigail the entire time.

My sister was pregnant - she found out the day after Abigail was born - but kept quiet for a few months to let Abigail be the only baby for a while.

The plan was to stay in Coulterville at Dad's house overnight. But we wanted to go home. We've wanted to go home for the past 23 days. Now that we were an hour away only extreme fatigue would stop us.

We said our goodbyes, loaded up on caffeine at the convenience store and headed home.

Our other babies, the cats, stayed in the basement this entire time. Relax, our basement was bigger than my first apartment. We asked our house-sitter to let them up from their basement home the day before.

When I walked in with our luggage, two of them sat by the dining room table and watched who came in. I called their names. When Warlock saw me, he stalked toward me. I petted his head as Esther came in with the baby.

By the time I moved the car to the garage and came back inside; Esther sat on the floor as the cats rubbed against her and the baby seat. Warlock sniffed at Abigail. Abigail stared back. I snapped a quick photo. The caption: "What the hell are you," each asked the other.

⌣⌢

The legalities weren't quite through. Later that month we headed back to Chicago to appear in court. We drove ourselves.

Pretty typical of coastal types: "You're from Illinois, ergo you must be from Chicago." No. Look at a map. Look how LONG Illinois is. Chicago can be a six-to-seven hour drive. The agency used an attorney from Chicago not knowing that. No one knows that. Well, no one that's not from southern or central Illinois knows that.

I lived in Carbondale when the football Cardinals left St. Louis. Carbondale is near the southern part of Illinois. Not at the very southern tip – it is still an hour away from the river-border. My Chicago friends said I needed to root for the Bears because they were from my home state.

"Home state? Chicago is to the rest of Illinois what North Dakota is to Guam."

"Well, it's the closest city with a football team."

"Indianapolis is."

"Second closest then."

"Kansas City."

"Wh …"

"Then Cincinnati." Nowadays we can put Memphis in there too.

So driving to Chicago to go to court was … inconvenient. But it made for a nice long weekend. We stayed in a nice hotel overnight and had dinner with my cousin and her husband. Abigail awoke a few times in the night for feeding and then it was up at six to get ready for court.

I had never been in the towering courthouse complex in Chicago. We went through security and to the floor where they held the adoption hearings.

We finally got to meet our attorney. She was very friendly and told us how pretty Abigail was. She took our papers to the clerk's office and Abigail was "served" summons – the clerk touched Abigail's forehead with the papers as our attorney took our picture. He gave her a plastic badge in the shape of the Cook County Sheriff's Office. Well, he put it on her blanket – she slept the entire time. We kept the badge - here's something unique she can take to show-and-tell.

I was excited at being in the same room where they filmed one of the scenes from "The Blues Brothers"! Well, it looked like the same room – it was definitely the same building!

We took more pictures of the beautiful skyline and the more-beautiful Esther and Abigail in the foreground.

We waited our turn in a playroom along with an older couple adopting a teenager, a couple with two other children adopting a four-year-old from Venezuela, and a same-sex couple adopting an infant a few months older than Abigail. We didn't chat among ourselves – the family of five played and chatted with each other. The rest of us were too nervous or too tired.

Now we got into the legal niceties of adoption that I remembered from the one I did in the early 1990s.

A guardian ad litem was appointed – Abigail's own attorney who would more or less recommend whatever the caseworker (remember Helen?) advised with rare exception. We appeared in front of a judge and asked if we agree to adopt the baby. Yes. Have we made provisions for wills and powers-of-attorney? Yes. Do we have a plan to take care of her in case something should happen to us? Yes. The judge asked what we did for a living. She asked what kind of law I practiced and had I done adoptions? Not for over fifteen years, I said.

We were appointed Abigail's guardians. There were two more home studies that Helen had to do and submit to the court and to the guardian ad litem. Helen hurt her leg and it was difficult for her to get around, but she managed to get the home study done and the paperwork filed.

On June 16th, 2010 the Honorable Judge Karkula signed the following Order from the Circuit Court of Cook County, Illinois: IT IS THEREFORE ORDERED, ADJUDGED AND DECREED that from this day the minor (child) shall, to all legal intents and purposes, be the child of (Michael and Esther Curry) … IT IS FURTHER ORDERED that the name of the child be, and is hereby changed to ABIGAIL SHELDON MARYJEAN CURRY…

The findings said I was of sound mind. There, it's official. A court of competent jurisdiction has so held. Take that, former girlfriends …

Also on June 16th, 2010 my sister gave birth to a baby girl. As with the call allowing us to go home; if I had made up that coincidence for a story, an editor would slash it out.

Esther and I always celebrated June 17th as "I Love You Day". It was halfway to Esther's birthday and the anniversary of her first marriage. And with our anniversary, both birthdays (now three birthdays) and Christmas all in the last part of the year; we wanted something to celebrate in the summer.

Now we call June 16th and 17th "Abby Day" or "Adoption Day". Some adoption advocates like to call it "Gotcha Day", but that sounds like something that would trigger an Amber Alert.

"Gotcha Day" is the day the parents receive the child into their custody. It can also be a substitute for when the real birthday is unknown. We know her birth date. And her "Gotcha Day" was two days later, so there is no point for us to have a "Gotcha Day". We like our two-day "Abby Day" holiday.

⌢

*B*ut that is all in the future.

On Sunday, October 11th, 2009 we were home after 23 long days away. Our life had changed irreversibly. One chapter closed and another started – as it had on our wedding day.

We put Abigail in her bassinette and went to bed. I awoke hours later thinking the baby was choking, but it was only Mau the cat sitting on our comforter giving us a welcome-home hairball.

The next day Esther was on the couch with cats Fizzy and Mau jockeying for position on her lap. Abigail snuggled on my chest, Warlock the cat on my right side and Nebula the cat on my left. I sat in my comfy green chair with my feet propped high. My chair, my home, my family. Life is … zzzzzzzzzzzz …

Epilogue

She is four years old now. She climbs onto my lap and lays her head on my chest. She puts her forehead against my neck. "My baby," she says. Using toddler logic she learned that this is what you say when you snuggle with someone. It's what her daddy says to her, after all...

"My baby," I say. I tell her the Baby Story, although that's mommy's story - she prefers I tell her the story of the kitty-cats watching the Clown Parade - including Daddy dressed as a pirate and a guest appearance by Santa at the end. Everyone throws candy. How she loves candy.

My baby.

Where was Abby on January 1st, 2009, when adoption first entered my mind? Was she conceived yet? Was she an embryo? A zygote? A single diploid cell? Or was she not even a gleam in the birth-parents' eyes?

The typical gestation period for a human is 38-42 weeks. Counting back from her birth date, early January is within that window. If I count back from the original estimate (September 23rd), it is likely she was conceived by then.

I don't really believe in ghosts or dragons or aliens, although I love to read and write about them. If proof of alien contact was found or if a corpse of a Bigfoot or a Nessie was found and verified, I would be tickled. I love stuff like that, although I don't believe in it.

But it's fun to imagine: Abby's little essence shooting through the ether a thousand miles to my and Esther's minds, saying, "Adopt. Adopt ME!" Then she sent messages to her birth-mother: "Put me up for adoption, my mommy and daddy are waiting."

But then my mind makes things even more complicated as we snuggle and watch Barney sing about butterflies for the umpteenth time.

Time.

Time is not a line or a winding river. Nor is it a big ball of wibbly-wobbly-timey-wimey stuff. Although that is probably closer to the truth.

I think time is an hourglass. Millions of grains of events swirling toward one singular event; that event then joins millions of other grains of events.

I think of all the swirling grains of events that led to our adopting Abigail.

Both Esther and I and Valerie picked the same adoption law firm.

Esther and I convinced our caseworker to allow a photograph taken over a year before, in violation of their rules, to place in our portfolio. Or did we? Was Abby tickling the caseworker's mind? "Let them include that photo!"

Valerie was attracted to that particular picture; one of the reasons "she" picked us.

I think of the grains of events leading to that one event – the taking of a photograph we will always treasure: Clyde and Virginia decided to have a twentieth wedding ceremony; decided on a renaissance/fantasy theme. They decided to pick Esther and me as the Matron of Honor and Best Man.

Our mutual friend Doug was the minister who renewed their vows. Doug introduced me to Esther back in 1996. He was the one who took that photo of us in front of the castle wall.

If he had not taken the picture; if he had not agreed to officiate at the wedding; if he had not introduced Esther and I ...

Older grains of sand – Clyde and Virginia getting married in 1984, whatever instilled a love of Tolkienesque fantasy in myself, Clyde, Esther and Virginia (and Doug) that would link us as friends.

What about all eight parents who did whatever they did (or didn't do what they should have done) that made us fall in love with Tolkienesque fantasy. So much so that Clyde and Virginia would use that as the theme for the renewing of their vows. So much so that Esther and I participated in full period dress.

Abby's been a busy girl these last fifty years. She has enough foresight and ability to tweak events that would make the Illuminati and the Bilderberg Group jealous.

OK, maybe not the Bilderberg Group ... forget I mentioned them. They don't exist of course...

What was that noise? Is someone there…?

So was Abby floating around us in January 2009 tugging on this strand and that; convincing us to move in certain directions? No.

Is it nice to think about it? Yes.

Is there a little Abby snuggling half-asleep on my lap watching Barney singing Mr. Sun for the eighth time this morning? Yes.

Is it nice to think about it? Oh yes.

I've been picked by a sweet and beautiful lady to be the love of her life.

Twice.

What a lucky man I am.

THE END

Thank you for reading my book. If you enjoyed it, won't you please take a moment to leave me a review at your favorite retailer?

Thanks!

Michael Curry

About the Author

Michael Curry is an attorney living in southern Illinois with his beloved wife and daughter. Michael plays a poor guitar and enjoys listening to British Invasion rock. He also collects - and reads - comic books from the 1960s and 1970s. Groovy. He writes - and reads - science fiction, fantasy and horror (thriller) short stories and novels.

Connect with Me:

Follow me on Twitter: http://twitter.com/currymichaelg
Friend me on Facebook: https://www.facebook.com/Michaelcurryauthor
Subscribe to my blog: http://michaelgcurry.blogspot.com or
http://michaelgcurry.com/curry-takeaways-blog/
Please visit my website: http://michaelgcurry.com/

Other books by Michael Curry

*H*ere is the introduction of my latest work - <u>Toddler TV: A Befuddled Father's Guide to What the Kid is Watching</u>. It should be available in the coming months - please look for it! I hope you enjoy it!

⌒

*S*ome time back I posted on Facebook:

All three of us watched the Teletubbies for the first time. Abby called them RubberDubbers. It was very confusing - "The purple one is Jeff, the red one is Murray. I thought Anthony was blue not green." "Well, he DID start off as green." "Who's the yellow one?" "That's LaLa." "I thought LaLa retired due to health reasons and was replaced by Sam. Where's Mr. Greenjeans and the Moose?"

And then in the comments:

"And where was Grandfather Clock? Isn't there a tiger living in the clock? And a trolley? And where's the big yellow bird? I am so lost!"

Ironically just days later the family of Gus "Cosmo" Allegretti announced he died in July 2013 at age 86. He was one of the last major cast members of <u>Captain Kangaroo</u>. He played Dennis the Apprentice but also did the voice for Mr. Moose (I did not know that but now that I think about it – it sounded just like him!), the voice for Grandfather Clock and was the puppeteer for Bunny Rabbit. There are other cast members still alive – but they were more secondary characters compared to Dennis, Mr. Green Jeans and the good Captain.

The less said about Slim Goodbody the better…

This got me thinking about the television shows my daughter watches. I wondered if other fathers were as befuddled as I was in choice and content. Mothers aren't befuddled – they are omnipotent. Perhaps fathers could benefit from a guide to children's programming: a guide from one father to another. A guide told from the perspective of a veteran couch potato and TV watcher.

So they could learn from my mistakes …

⟨⟩

One month shy of my 45th birthday I became a father for the very first time. A beautiful girl with brown eyes and brown hair. Oh heavens, what have I gotten myself into…

We avoided television for her first year – we researched all the bad news about the electronic babysitter. We read books together and listened to music instead. As she got older, though, we watched TV programs with her. She recognized some of the characters from her books – Big Bird and Oscar the Grouch.

At the same time her babysitter let her watch TV, too. By the time my daughter was two she was into Dora, Barney and <u>Sesame Street</u>. She is now four years old and has her favorites and her not-so-favorites. She is officially an All-American-TV–Zombie. Just like her dad.

Children's television is a much broader landscape than it was when I was her age. I was born in late 1964. My first memory is my grandfather installing our swing set. My next memory is of the moon landing. I would have been just over 4½ years old. It was late, late at night – around 7:30 or so. I remember my parents telling me to watch this important thing happening on the TV. I remember that – their telling me to watch – more so than the event itself.

Still, I think that's what instilled my love of science, science fiction and all things nerdy.

I have two younger sisters. Among the many hang-ups that caused include watching children's television programs until 1982 or so, when I left for college. When I was four years old TV programs aimed at children were either Saturday morning cartoons or local programs with people dressed as clowns and/or people and their puppet cohorts showing syndicated cartoons and doing silly skits. Pie-throwing was frequently involved.

There was this thing called NET and PBS that aired educational programs for children, but there wasn't much to it compared to Bugs Bunny, the Groovie Ghoolies and HR Pufinstuf.

By the time I left the world of children's TV, PBS was fully ensconced in our American way of life. Sesame Street, Mr. Rogers' Neighborhood and The Electric Company were expected, if not mandatory, viewing. Captain Kangaroo was still around, but Zoom, Letter People and Villa Alegre were gone.

Romper Room was around until the 1990s, but it was long gone from my area. I don't know if the St. Louis version had its own host or showed the syndicated national program. At the time I had no idea what any of that meant. I was just waiting breathlessly for the host to mention my name. "Romper bomper stomper boo. Tell me, tell me, tell me do. Magic Mirror, tell me today, have all my friends had fun at play?" I sent in my name and my birth date. Naturally on my birthday I slept in and missed. It. "Did she say my name," I ask my mother. "Yes she did," she said. I suspect now she didn't and my mother said she did. Mom could handle the smaller explosion of my missing it better than handle the larger explosion of the host not mentioning me on my birthday. That I still remember that day forty-five years later …

There was no channel devoted solely to children's television, let alone three or four channels! My daughter has that choice now, though – Sprout, Disney Jr., Nick Jr., good old PBS, even a channel of Christian-themed kid shows called "Smchild" on the satellite. Kids were no longer relegated to Saturday mornings and before and after school. I don't know a toddler that watches TV at two in the morning, but their shows are on!

And that is the point of this little exercise. Toddler TV: a Befuddled Father's Guide to What the Kid is Watching is the result of my viewing, and PRE-viewing, most of the shows available for my daughter to watch.

"Hey," you might say, "you spend an entire chapter on Mr. Rogers and only one page to Spongebob! What the heck is that about?!" or "I was raised on Teenage Mutant Chili Peppers! Where are they in this stupid guide?!"

Good points. I focus on the preschool shows. Spongebob, although a good show, is aimed at kids older than mine. Sorry, but it's true. Preschoolers may watch Spongebob – and there are certainly toys and games aimed at them with that franchise stamp on it – but the show isn't aimed at them. It shouldn't be at any rate. And the Red Hot Ninja Turtles? Older kids still.

Remember – preschoolers.

If your favorite show is missing that may be the reason. Or I may not have the channel on which it airs. Or I may have simply forgotten. I'm almost fifty raising a baby for heaven's sake. I'm lucky I remember to dress each morning.

Do not forget this is done in the spirit of humor and love, even love for the shows I do not like all that much. You'll be able to tell which I like and which I don't. The shows are explained and critiqued not only for the children but the weary parent watching it, too.

Bonafides? Sorry, I'm a lawyer in real life and prone to using bigger words than necessary. "Bonafides" is a fancy-shmancy way of asking, "what qualifies you, Mr. Smarty?"

I wrote for (and had a small role in) a children's television show for a PBS affiliate in the 1980s. Our producers told us that we needed a few small nods to the parents watching to keep them, and ultimately the kids, interested. Give the grown-ups a wink – a joke or reference that will go over the children's heads but not theirs – and the parents will encourage their kids to keep watching. Sesame Street was a pro at that – especially Jim Henson via Kermit the Frog.

At that time the majority of Sesame Street's viewers were adults. Some adults watched the show without a toddler in sight. College students were a sizable chunk of the Street's audience.

The reason some kid shows are so despised is because they lack that connection with adults. Teletubbies & Barney & Friends are two examples of shows adults hate because there is nothing – nothing - aimed at them.

There was nothing aimed at adults in Mr. Roger's Neighborhood either, you might say. True, but as I will say later, MRN was an unmovable force. Parents were as mesmerized by its quiet and gentle-yet-firm demand to be respected as were the children.

Some shows are popular; other shows just as good or better are not. Some shows work; some do not. Maybe we can find out why. Let's see what the children are watching…